Collins

Burns Supper Companion

Nancy Marshall

HarperCollins*Publishers*

HarperCollins Publishers
Westerhill Road, Bishopbriggs, Glasgow G64 2QT

www.fireandwater.com

First published by W&R Chambers Ltd, Edinburgh in 1992
First published by HarperCollins in 2001

Reprint 10 9 8 7 6 5 4 3 2 1 0

ISBN 0 00 711858 9

A catalogue record for this book is available from The British Library.

Printed and bound in Great Britain by
Omnia Books Ltd, Glasgow

CONTENTS

For
Tori and Nina

PREFACE

This book has been written for those who have never been to a Burns Supper and also would rather not attend their first one without possessing any knowledge of the form or substance of such an occasion. The elaborate ritual of Burns Night can be mystifying to the newcomer. The following will hopefully shed some light on this old Scots tradition and enable it to be enjoyed to the full.

Here the form of a traditional Burns Supper is spelled out in simple terms according to the best authorities on the subject: the Burns Federation and some of the oldest Burns clubs in existence. In addition you will find material to help you organise your own supper or even deliver an 'Immortal Memory' speech, should you be willing to try.

An evening to celebrate the life and works of Robert Burns is a worthwhile way to share good company. It should be both serious and fun. If this volume helps you to do it with confidence, it will have served its purpose.

Nancy Marshall
Edinburgh, 2001

THE LIFE OF ROBERT BURNS
(1759-96)

BURNS — THE MAN AND THE POET

Robert Burns was born on 25 January 1759 in the Ayrshire village of Alloway. Most of the following 37 years, until his death in 1796, were spent working on the land, from farm labourer on his father's farms to farmer himself. Only during the last five years of his life, while acting as an exciseman in Dumfries, did he manage to free himself from the burden of toiling in the fields and even then, as he laid down the yoke of the soil for the last time, it was merely to travel the 200 miles a week on horseback needed to perform his excise duties. Life was never easy for Robert Burns. But whatever came his way, good or bad, pleasure or pain, he hungrily took it up like the artist he was, and celebrated the experience. His dogged determination in everything is reflected in the power of his work. Whether describing the instantaneous pleasure, the sad memory or the fleeting joy, he seems to capture and illuminate these feelings.

Burns's acute perception of life and everything and everyone around him originated in the early years he spent labouring on his father's farms. The fires of injustice were kindled in him as year after year of toil brought the family no relief from their daily hardship and the threat of the factor, and eviction for non-payment of rent always loomed in the background. The pain of these days, both physical and mental, was etched for ever into his mind. It was the source of his quicksilver mood changes, his depressions and melancholia. But more importantly it was the cradle of his creativity.

Robert Burns was a complex character, a loyal friend, a dangerous enemy with a fast, biting tongue, a caring and loving father, a hardworking farmer, a great debater who needed social stimulus as much as he craved the quiet and solitude of his own fireside; he was neither a fool as to how others saw him, nor was he the uneducated 'ploughman poet' he allowed himself to be mistaken for.

Burns drank, but probably no more to excess than was the norm for the day. He had a way with the ladies, but as he describes in 'Address to the Unco Guid, or the Rigidly Righteous', the only reason some resist temptation is that temptation is never put in their way. The power of his work has stood the test of time, the sentiments in it as valid today as they have ever been. He combined intellect with imagination and instinct, and never lost his sense of justice, which gave him the freedom to expound his beliefs and loudly proclaim life's pleasures and passions.

In a country being overrun by English ways and customs and English government, the average Scotsman in Burns's time felt his way of life slipping away. Writing in the everyday language still used by the mass of the population, Burns avowed that their culture was still alive and in so doing elevated their existence and their pride in that existence. The gap he filled was a mixture of hope for the future and a nostalgia for the past, rather like the sentiments expressed in 'Auld Lang Syne'.

FAMILY HISTORY

Robert Burns's father, William Burnes, settled in Ayrshire in 1750 but hailed originally from Kincardineshire, in the northeast of Scotland. His family had been tenant farmers on the estate of Earl Marischal, a staunch Stuart supporter. In later life, the romantic in Burns liked to believe that his ancestors' fall on hard times was due to their loyalty to the Jacobite cause, rather than such mundane reasons as his grandfather's over-ambitious farming ventures or a succession of bad harvests. Whatever the reasons, the Burnes's household was broken up in 1748 due to bankruptcy, and the sons, William and Robert, went elsewhere in search of work. The poet's father, William, walked to Edinburgh and found work as a gardener, being employed for a time in helping to lay out 'the Meadows'. In 1750 he moved to Ayrshire on the west coast of Scotland, where he continued as a gardener: first for the Laird of Fairlee, then with the Crawfords of Doonside and finally at Doonholm for Dr Fergusson. During this time, this determined, hardworking man put aside enough money to lease seven and a half acres of land in Alloway, where he planned to build a house and set up as a market gardener. He continued working at Doonholm, while he began his market garden, and in 1757, just seven years after his arrival in Ayrshire, during the summer and autumn, he built, with his own hands, the 'auld clay biggin' known all over the world today as Burns Cottage. It was intended as a home for his bride Agnes Brown, the daughter of an Ayrshire tenant farmer, whom he married on 15 December 1757. By then William Burnes was 36 years of age and his new wife 25. He was a slim, wiry figure of medium height and she was a small, vivacious redhead. They both possessed strong tempers,

Burns Cottage

both had the ethos of hard work stamped through them and, probably because of their 'late' marriage, they both brought maturity and stability to a relationship which survived happily until William's death in 1784. Robert, the first of their seven children, was born on 25 January 1759.

ALLOWAY

In Alloway the family's life passed pleasantly. While William Burnes continued to work as a gardener and run his small market garden, his wife looked after the dairy, and along with her cousin, Betty Davidson, entertained the children with old Scottish songs and tall tales, which unbeknown to them, were to stimulate Burns's imagination and influence his work all his days. In 1765, at the age of six, and with his younger brother Gilbert, Robert entered the village school of Alloway for his first formal education. Unfortunately after little more than a month, the schoolmaster left for Ayr and the school closed. An ever-resourceful William Burnes quickly got together with the heads of four other families and found a new master for the school, arranging that they split the cost of his salary between them and take it in turns to board him.

MOUNT OLIPHANT

John Murdoch, the young man who filled the post, regarded Robert and Gilbert as bright and hardworking. Gilbert of the two he thought had a 'more lively imagination' and was 'more of the wit, than Robert', and musically he found 'Robert's ear, in particular, was remarkably dull, and his voice untunable'. Murdoch continued to teach the boys for a time, although only sporadically, after the family moved to Mount Oliphant Farm early in 1766. By then William Burnes thought the cottage too small for his growing family and, to prevent his children becoming labourers and therefore 'underlings' in another household, he leased Mount Oliphant, a few miles from Alloway, at £40 per year, becoming a tenant farmer like his ancestors. And he was to fare no better. In these 70 acres of exhausted soil, which hardly covered the rocks beneath, the family toiled in backbreaking work and lived in extreme frugality for the next 12 years. During that time, Robert performed a man's work, when he was still little more than a child, and in the process irreversibly damaged his heart. He described his time there as being 'the cheerless gloom of a hermit, with the unceasing moil of a galley slave'. Gilbert believed that Robert's later melancholia and the depressions which haunted him all his adult life stemmed from this time. Describing Robert's physical condition he said, 'At this time he was almost constantly afflicted in the evenings with a dull headache, which, at a subsequent period of his life, was exchanged for a palpitation of the heart, and a threatening of fainting and suffocation in the night time.' Robert's drastic measures to stop the palpitations included keeping a bucket of water at his bedside into which he plunged his head in the hope of relieving the spasm.

During these years William Burnes, when not teaching Robert and Gilbert himself, and instructing them on the Bible, periodically sent them to different schools to brush up on their work. It shows the remarkable strength and character of this kindly, but stern father that even while trying to eke out an existence for the family and contend with threatening letters from the factor over unpaid rent, he still found the time and inclination to foster the future for his children.

By the age of 18 Robert, a compulsive reader from his earliest days, had devoured the works of Shakespeare, Milton, Dryden, Gray, Shenstone, Pope and Addison. Apart from the fiction of Henry Fielding and Tobias Smollett and the philosophy and history of David Hume and William Robertson, he knew intimately the works of his predecessors in Scottish literature, Allan Ramsay and Robert Fergusson, he read French and had a little Latin. The

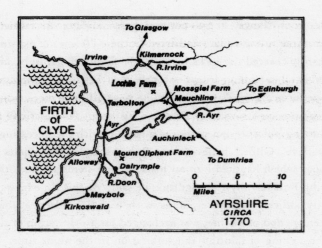

Bible, as he was to depict in 'The Cotter's Saturday Night', was standard reading for any God-fearing Scottish family. It was hardly the background of an 'unlettered ploughman'.

LOCHLIE

In 1777 Robert's horizons widened immeasurably when his father decided to take the lease of Lochlie Farm, three miles from Mauchline and two and a half miles from Tarbolton. In farming terms, it was little better a bargain than Mount Oliphant, either financially (the rent was high at £1 for each of the 130 acres) or in soil condition. William Burnes had merely exchanged poor, exhausted soil for swampy, undrained land, but for the next four years his family enjoyed a more comfortable lifestyle and Robert found new friends and stimulating company in the nearby farms and villages. It was here that he set out to mark himself as different by tying his hair back unlike the other men of the parish, who traditionally wore their hair short. In 1780 the Tarbolton Bachelors' Club was founded and Robert became one of its leading lights, delighting in the debates and gaining confidence from the fierce interchange of passions and personalities. His hand can be detected in the rules, which were drawn up:

> No haughty, self-conceited person, who looks upon himself as superior to the rest of the club, and especially no mean-spirited worldly mortal, whose only will is to heap up money, shall upon any pretence whatever be admitted.

By the following year Burns had become a Freemason in St David's Lodge, Tarbolton, and it was due to this early masonic commitment that he found his later entry into Edinburgh made easier. The ladies had by then also begun to interest him: in his earlier youth the charms of Nellie Kilpatrick and Peggy Thomson had disturbed him, and now at 22 he developed an attachment to Alison Begbie, a farmer's daughter. She turned down his offer of marriage and, depressed and dejected, Burns went off to Irvine to learn the art of flax-dressing. He did set up in business with a partner, but the venture failed. His great friend from the Irvine days was Richard Brown, a sailor and great ladies' man, who, if the stories are to be believed, led Burns astray with his libidinous attitude to women. But more importantly, he was the first person to suggest that Robert become a poet.

On his return to Lochlie early in 1782, Burns found his father involved in litigation with the factor over arrears in rent. The weather had been bad and consequently the harvests poor, and this combined with a general downturn in the economy toppled many small Ayrshire farmers of that period. By the time the sheriff's officers came to the farm to sell their cattle, tools and crops on 17 May 1783, William Burnes was ill with consumption and physically frail after all his years of hard labour. It seems that Burns developed an acute hatred of the landowning classes after years of watching his father being tormented by their factors making demands for money he could not find:

this final sequestration of all their goods and chattels strengthened Robert's belief that all men should share the same rights and privileges. William Burnes died at Lochlie on 17 February 1784 and was buried in Alloway Kirkyard, the scene of Tam o' Shanter's nightmare encounter with the witches.

MOSSGIEL

Burns's spirit was maybe embittered by life's inequalities, but his brain was as sharp as ever, and in the autumn of 1783, some five months before his father's death, he and Gilbert arranged to rent Mossgiel Farm to provide, as Gilbert later described it, 'an asylum for the family in case of the worst'. They also shrewdly claimed against their father's bankrupt estate as employees, and with this money and whatever savings the family had, after William Burnes's death, removed to Mossgiel, where Robert became head of the family. It was at this point that the 'e' was dropped from their surname. Mossgiel, a 118-acre property with an annual rent of £90, lay one mile from Mauchline and, with its heavy clay soil and high elevation, it was to prove no better a bargain than the previous farms, even though Robert was determined to make it a success. However, the combination of a new-found independence and responsibility as head of the family seemed to release in him an enormous creative force. True, he had begun his First Commonplace Book at Lochlie, in which he jotted down ideas, thoughts and impressions about life, while he continued to write both poetry and prose. Now, here at Mossgiel between the years of 1784 and 1786, he produced work of such exceptional calibre that had he never written another word, he would still have been recognised as a great poet.

The ecclesiastical satires 'Holy Willie's Prayer', 'Address to the Deil' and 'The Holy Fair', come from this time, as do 'The Twa Dogs', 'To a Mouse',

'The Jolly Beggars', 'The Cotter's Saturday Night' and 'Address to the Unco Guid'.

But, apart from this prolific output and the strain of working the farm, Robert also found time for new and influential friends, such as his landlord, Gavin Hamilton, and the lawyer, Robert Aiken of Ayr. John Richmond, one of Gavin Hamilton's clerks, and James Smith, a local draper, together with Burns made up a well-known trio in Mauchline, enjoying many evenings in the Whiteford Inn or Poosie Nansie's. His reputation as a poet was well known locally, but his fame was spreading too amongst 'the Belles of Mauchline'. In May 1785, his first illegitimate child, a daughter, was born to Elizabeth Paton, one of the servants on the farm, and by the end of the same year he had wooed and won Jean Armour; their first set of twins was born the following September.

Both these events brought down the wrath of the Kirk Session of Mauchline Parish Church on the poet's head: he had to appear publicly in church to be condemned for the sin of fornication. This was common practice in Scotland at that time, but for Burns it was a bitter humiliation, especially in the case of Jean Armour. After his initial delight at her pregnancy and his written promise of marriage (then recognised as a legal and binding contract), he was shattered to find that Jean's father, totally opposed to the match, had taken steps to have both of their names cut out of the document. Burns's anger and bitterness were reserved for Jean; in his eyes, by handing over the paper to her father, she had betrayed him.

But James Armour, master mason and respected citizen of Mauchline, was not yet finished with the local rhyming rake. In the early summer of 1786, in the knowledge that Burns was in the process of publishing what is now known as the Kilmarnock edition of his poems, he determined to have a financial settlement for Jean and had a warrant issued against the poet for a substantial sum of money. But wily Burns had calculated his actions and had already signed his share of Mossgiel over to Gilbert, ostensibly for the support of Betty Paton's child and included 'the profits that may arise from the publication of my poems presently in the press'.

Burns continued to agonise over Jean and what he saw as her appalling treatment of him, but true to form, in the middle of this turmoil, he turned to Mary Campbell, better known today as 'Highland Mary'. In May of that year he proceeded to offer her marriage, while thinking about emigrating to Jamaica to work as a bookkeeper. Whether he was planning to take Mary with him is a matter of conjecture, as is the reason for her death in October of that same year. It was said to have been caused by typhus although many rumours circulated that she had died in childbirth. There is no evidence of either. 'Afton Water' was written in her memory.

EDINBURGH

On 31 July 1786 the Kilmarnock edition of Burns's work was published and in one month the total 612 copies were sold out; public response was deafening and his poems were read from cottage to castle. The literary world was stunned by the extraordinary talent of this supposed 'unlettered ploughman'. On 3 September Jean Armour gave birth to twins, a boy and girl. Burns left Mossgiel on 27 November for what was to be the first of two winters spent in Edinburgh. It must be remembered that he did not arrive in Edinburgh either friendless, socially inept or intellectually inferior. John Richmond, his friend from Mauchline, now lived there, his masonic affiliations brought many useful contacts, the *literati* fêted him after their 'master' Henry Mackenzie's applause and 'society' drooled over him when the Earl of Glencairn gave his seal of approval. His dress was restrained, his conversation sharp, satirical and decisive, his wit unmatched. His instincts fortunately overruled the often proferred advice to tone down the Scots in his work and, while there is no doubt that he thoroughly enjoyed the fuss he created, in the midst of the social whirl, this well-educated, well-read ploughman, with his feet firmly on the ground, never lost sight of his novelty value. He described his situation in a letter to a friend:

> 'When proud fortune's ebbing tide recedes' – you may bear me witness, when my bubble of fame was at the highest, I stood, unintoxicated, with the inebriating cup in my hand, looking forward, with rueful resolve, to the hastening time when the stroke of envious Calumny, with all the eagerness of vengeful triumph, should dash it to the ground.
>
> *(Letter to Rev. William Greenfield, December 1786)*

On the other hand Edinburgh did provide him with convivial company, such as the Crochallan Fencibles, a drinking club of lawyers and merchants, who met regularly at a tavern in Anchor Place. It was here that Burns met Alexander Cunningham, an Edinburgh lawyer, who proved to be a good and loyal friend to him during his lifetime and a great support to Jean Armour after Burns's death. The connections he made in the capital also helped to further his ambition of becoming an excise officer and Patrick Miller, a banker in the city, offered him the lease on Ellisland Farm in Dumfriesshire. Most importantly he saw a second edition of his poems published, a run of some 3000 copies, on 21 April 1787 by William Creech. A notorious skinflint, Creech cunningly bought the copyright for 100 guineas and managed to hold back payment for sales and subscriptions for another two years. Burns turned down the offer of Ellisland Farm, although he did visit there during his tour of the Borders in May of that year. At this point in his life he saw a return to farming as a step back into backbreaking toil and poverty; he therefore pushed for an excise position, enlisting all the influence he could muster, while friends assured him that a ploughman he was and a ploughman he should stay.

SCOTTISH TOURS

During the rest of 1787 Burns journeyed quite extensively through Scotland. Apart from his Borders tour, in June he travelled to Argyll to the west Highlands and in August he began a three-week trip around the Highlands with his friend William Nicol, staying with the Duke and Duchess of Athole at Blair Castle, dining at Castle Gordon at Fochabers, visiting Culloden Moor, the scene of the last Jacobite stand, and the site of the Battle of Bannockburn. In October, in the company of Dr James Adair, he visited Stirling on the way to Harvieston in Clackmannanshire to stay with the Chalmers family. Relatives of Gavin Hamilton, Burns had met and admired their daughter Peggy before, and he now proposed marriage to her but was turned down.

Meanwhile, in July of that same year, between these trips Burns returned to Mossgiel and found James Armour with an entirely different view of him. Now that the father of Jean's twins was a famous, celebrated and, he assumed, soon to be wealthy poet, he was a decidedly different catch from the unsuccessful farmer and local scribbler that Jean's father had previously refused. Putting aside his irritation with James Armour's new-found friendship and the feelings of resentment at Jean's 'betrayal', Burns visited her and their children. Jean, once again seduced by his charm, produced their second set of twins the following March. Sadly both children died within a few weeks of their birth.

CLARINDA

The 'Clarinda' episode from December 1787 until the following spring was a curious hiatus in Burns's life, apart from the now famous correspondence between them and the beautiful love song 'Ae Fond Kiss', it appears to have suspended him from reality for a time.

Burns met Agnes (Nancy) McLehose at a tea party in Miss Erskine Nimmo's home in Edinburgh in early December. The same age as Burns, married, but separated from her husband, she was the mother of three small children. Petite, blonde, with a spontaneous manner, she was not what Burns was accustomed to meeting in the drawing rooms of Edinburgh, a world away from the reticent felicity of the Edinburgh lady. He was bowled over by the interest she showed in his work. Quick to bring him to her side, she established a common ground in their mutual knowledge and love of literature and mentioned her own dabbling in 'amateur poetics'. Determined to have an invite to tea that day, she'd read his poetry, heard the gossip and now that he was here in front of her she wasted no time in inviting him to take tea with her later that week.

Fate was to take a hand and their next meeting was delayed. Travelling in a coach which overturned, Burns was left with a dislocated knee. This is when the famous correspondence began. By the time they did meet again in early January, Burns had built himself up into a frenzy over the beguiling Mrs McLehose. Writing to Richard Brown on 30th December he declared:

> Love still "reigns and revels" in my bosom; and I am at this moment ready to hang myself for a young Edinburgh widow, who has wit and beauty more murderously fatal than the assassinating stiletto of the Sicilian Banditti.

Imagine his disappointment when he was made to realise that conversation, poetry and letters were all that was to be exchanged and that his 'Clarinda', because of her rigid Calvinist upbringing, would not be falling prey to the 'persuasions' of Rob Mossgiel. Still Burns believed he could break down the barriers. 'An hour in the dark with Rob is worth a lifetime with any other lad', was how the lasses of Ayrshire described him.

Agnes Craig's father had been a prominent surgeon in Glasgow and it was here at the age of eighteen that the young lawyer James McLehose persuaded her to marry him. Her family, dubious about the match at the time, were later proved right as he went on to become a notorious drunk and gambler. After a spell in debtors' prison in London, his well-connected family, to save any further embarrassment, had him sent to Jamaica. He made no provision for his wife and children and in 1782, when her father died leaving her a small annuity, Agnes McLehose moved to Edinburgh into the first floor of a house at the back of General's Entry in Potterrow, where the family lived genteelly, supported by kind friends and influential relatives.

Throughout history it has been easy to portray Nancy McLehose as a pretty, vain woman, who had her head turned by the great poet. Not so. Nancy, although self-taught, was well-read, eager to learn and improve. She was forthright and strong-minded in her views and could quote, at length, from both poetry and prose, a facility she retained almost to the end of her life. She was proficient, if not gifted, in poetry. Burns had her 'To a Blackbird Singing on a Tree' published in Johnson's *Scots Musical Museum*. At her suggestion he tidied it up and added some lines of his own. No doubt he enjoyed flexing his literary muscles in helping Nancy to improve her verse.

It is easier still to infer their relationship was not as purely platonic as Mrs McLehose insisted it was. The line 'Sylvander, you saw Clarinda last night, behind the scenes!' from her agitated letter of 13th January and the phrase 'behind the scenes', in particular, has been seized upon by some biographers as evidence that the affair was consummated. This is pure conjecture and there has never been any proof one way or the other. What we do know is that Nancy was well aware of the 'slant' which might be put upon their friendship. Early in their correspondence it was she who suggested they adopt the names Clarinda and Sylvander and, yes, adopting Arcadian terms added a certain romance to their correspondence (and allowed a step back from reality) but it also, to an extent, protected the identities of the writers should their letters be intercepted. As she points out in a P.S. to her letter of December 21st: 'I entreat you not to mention our correspondence to one on earth. Though I have conscious innocence, my situation is a delicate one.'

Clarinda and Sylvander were well matched in their letter writing skills, both knowing how and when to turn up the emotional heat and bring the other to heel. From the initial modest overture of mutual admiration:

> I can say with truth, Madam, that I have never met with a person in my life whom I more anxiously wished to meet again than yourself.
>
> *(Sylvander to Clarinda, December 8th.)*

> Miss Nimmo can tell you how earnestly I had long pressed her to make us acquainted. I had a presentiment that we should derive pleasure from the society of each other.
>
> *(Clarinda to Sylvander in her reply the same day)*

through intense declarations:

> Do not be displeased when I tell you I wish our parting was over. At a distance we shall retain the same heartfelt affection and

interestedness in each other's concerns; but absence will mellow and restrain those violent heart-agitations, which, if continued much longer, would unhinge my very soul, and render me unfit for the duties of life.'

(Clarinda to Sylvander, January 24th)

Oh Love and Sensibility, ye have conspired against my Peace! I love to madness, and I feel to torture! Clarinda, how can I forgive myself, that I have ever touched a single chord in your bosom with pain! Would I do it willingly? Would any consideration, any gratification, make me do so? Oh, did you love like me, you could not deny or put off a meeting with the man who adores you; – who would die a thousand deaths before he would injure you; and who must soon bid you a long farewell!

(Sylvander to Clarinda, January 25th)

to the final 'warring sighs and groans' of 'Ae Fond Kiss'.

During these few months from December until April they exchanged 82 letters, on some days two were sent in each direction. And Burns's regular visits to her home were noticed; in one of her letters she urges him to be discreet: – 'Come to tea if you please, but eight will be a better hour less liable to intrusions, I hope you'll come afoot, even though you take a chair home. A chair is so uncommon a thing in our neighbourhood, it is apt to raise speculation – but they are all asleep by ten.' These visits caused so much gossip that friends and relatives, including her cousin the judge Lord Craig, advised her to stop seeing him. Burns, incensed at their meddling, increased his assurances of devotion.

An escape and indulgence for them both? Yes. But it's not difficult to see why. Midwinter, dreich, grey. A pretty, vulnerable woman, a smooth-tongued charmer pressing his suit, she resisting him, he resisting his obligations to Jean Armour, unsure and unconvinced about a future in print, believing the chance of an excise post was no more than just that, loath to take on the lease at Ellisland. There is no doubt Burns was bewitched. But it ran deeper than that. Clarinda, for him, was the embodiment of another kind of life far away from the gruelling toil of farming. He knew it was a life he would never have a share in and deep down he also knew it was a life in which he would never be comfortable. He realised his time in Edinburgh was up, the novelty of the 'ploughman poet' wearing off, his star, as he had predicted, on the wane

With the spring came reality. With heavy heart and determined chin he went back to the land and his responsibilities. He agreed to the lease on Ellisland in March, the same month as Jean gave birth to their second set of twins. In April he made her his wife by mutual declaration, a legal contract at that time. It is clear from the letters that Nancy knew about Jean Armour and both pregnancies. Burns even wrote to Clarinda from Ayrshire in early March, just days before the twins were born, decrying Jean, praising Clarinda. He delayed telling his friend Bob Ainslie, an Edinburgh lawyer, knowing he would take the bad tidings to Nancy. It was not until 26 May that he wrote to tell him. Presumably Ainslie did break the news to Nancy, when we don't know, but it was not until ten months later in March 1789 that she wrote a less than loving missive to Burns accusing him of villainy. The year after Burns's death Bob Ainslie managed to retrieve some of her letters from Alexander Cunningham and she destroyed this and many others. Burns decided to fight fire with fire and replied adopting an indignant tone, managing to completely ignore Jean's predicament at that point in time, asserting that during his stay in Edinburgh he was not under 'the smallest moral tie to Mrs Burns'. He goes on in mock-frustration to flatter her:

Was I to blame, Madam, in being the distracted victim of charms which, I affirm it, no man ever approached with impunity? Had I seen the least glimmering of hope that these charms could ever have been mine; or even had not iron necessity — But these are unavailing words.

In December 1791 Clarinda and Sylvander met again in Edinburgh. She'd written him a frosty note ostensibly to ask for his help for Jenny Clow, who had been one of her servants. It seems that while Burns was romancing her employer Jenny was providing solace of a different kind. She had produced a son in November 1788. Burns had acknowledged the boy as his at the time and offered, as he did on other occasions, to take the boy back home to be brought up by Jean. Jenny had refused. Now as she lay dying from tuberculosis, living in mean conditions, Nancy urged him to provide some basic necessities for her, finishing with the chill:

You have now an opportunity to evince you indeed possess these fine feelings you have delineated, so as to claim that just admiration of your country. I am convinced I need add nothing farther to persuade you to act as every consideration of humanity as well as gratitude must dictate. I am, Sir, your sincere well-wisher,

A.M.

Burns answered the summons and came to Edinburgh, the promise of seeing Nancy, no matter how angry, uppermost in his mind. He ate humble pie, visited Jenny and provided money for her care. She died the following month. When he returned to Dumfries it was without his son. Whether Jenny again refused or Burns didn't offer is not clear. The boy went on to become a successful Edinburgh merchant.

If Burns's reason for coming to Edinburgh was two-fold, so was Nancy's in asking him. She had agreed with her husband to try for a reconciliation and planned to sail to Jamaica the following February. This might be the last chance she would have to see the poet. At this meeting they kissed, exchanged locks of hair (Burns had hers enclosed in a ring) and healed the old wounds. They agreed to begin writing again, although Nancy was keen to place things on a different footing and modify the sentiments. Burns had difficulty containing himself. The Arcadian names were dropped and to some extent the letters are less effusive, but only by degree. Burns returned to Dumfries after this, their final encounter, wrote 'Ae Fond Kiss' and sent it to her.

In August of that same year Nancy McLehose returned from Jamaica. She had arrived to find her husband unchanged in his habits and the father of several other children. She didn't contact Burns when she returned, realising their relationship was over, too embarrassed to tell him what she'd found. James McLehose died in Kingston in 1812, rich in these later years, but he still refused to support his wife and children.

There were no letters between them during her stay in the West Indies. They had arranged to keep in contact through Mary Peacock, a friend of Nancy's, but somehow none of Burns's letters ever arrived. On 6 December 1792, the anniversary of their final meeting, Burns tried again and this time Mary Peacock did reply, but, in turn, this letter was 'mislaid' in the house in Wee Vennel, Dumfries and only turned up months later lying behind a chest of drawers. With the long letter of March 1793, chiding her for ignoring him, neglecting to let him know she had returned, Burns enclosed a two-volume copy of his latest work just published by Creech. There is no record of a reply.

In June 1794 finding himself alone one night in the Douglas Arms Hotel in Castle Douglas and out of favour with another "amateur poetess' Maria

Riddell, Burns wrote a sad, rambling note to his Clarinda:

> You would laugh, were you to see me, where I am just now: would to Heaven you were here to laugh with me, though I am afraid that crying would be our first employment. – Here I am set, a solitary hermit, in the solitary room, of a solitary inn, with a solitary bottle of wine by me –

> Before you ask me why I have not written to you first let me be informed of you, *how*, I shall write to you. 'In Friendship,' you say; & I have many a time taken up my pen to try to write an epistle of 'Friendship' to you; but it will not do: 'tis like Jove grasping a pop-gun, after having wielded his thunder. – When I take up the pen, Recollection ruins me. Ah! my ever dearest Clarinda! – Clarinda? What a host of Memory's tenderest offspring crowd on my fancy at that sound! – But I must not indulge that subject; you have forbid it.

He went on to declare that whenever and wherever he was called upon to give a toast it was to her:

> I constantly give you; but as your name has never passed my lips, even to my most intimate friend, I give you by the name of Mrs. Mack. Ah my dearest Clarinda!

After this display of continued adoration Burns, in his best shooting-himself-in-the-foot style, finished off by castigating Maria Riddell for her cruelty to him and enclosed a spiteful poem about her. Clarinda never replied. This was the last correspondence between them.

Nancy McLehose lived out the rest of her life in Edinburgh, dying there in 1841 at the age of 82. She enjoyed a busy social life with a wide circle of friends, and invitations to her New Year's Day suppers were much sought after. She had been a loving and indulgent mother to her children, as is evident in her letters to Burns, although sadly only one son survived childhood. He died in 1839, two years before Nancy's death, and all his family, except one grandson, predeceased him. Nancy's religious beliefs remained strong throughout her life, supporting her as she grew frail and infirm in old age. Increasing deafness then caused her to withdraw from society, and with many of her friends already gone she ended her days quietly and simply. During these latter years she altered some of the more ardent passages in Burns's letters before showing them to friends and eventually had to sell some for a few shillings in order to support herself. She never forgot her Sylvander. In her journal of 6 December 1831 she wrote: 'This day I never can forget. Parted with Burns in the year 1791, never more to meet in this world – Oh may we meet in Heaven!'

Sir Walter Scott believed that the fourth verse of 'Ae Fond Kiss' was 'the essence of a thousand love tales'. It was that and more. The yearning in this final farewell to Clarinda signifies not only the pain of a lost love, but is also an elegy to his lost hope.

> Had we never lov'd sae kindly!
> Had we never lov'd sae blindly!
> Never met – or never parted,
> We had ne'er been broken-hearted.

DUMFRIESSHIRE

To the south from Burns's native Ayrshire, beyond the counties of Kyle and Carrick, lies the old Scottish 'kingdom' of Galloway. Ruled by the Lords of Galloway until the mid-15th century this secluded, south west corner of Scotland was home to covenanters, smugglers, superstition and witchcraft.

By the end of the 18th century the area had a rich agrarian economy, exporting livestock and cereals to ports in England, Ireland and abroad. In the small towns and villages, apart from the established industries of ship-building and quarrying, there was plentiful evidence of commercial investment in the form of tanneries, distilleries, breweries, wood and metal workshops and latterly textile mills producing woollen and cotton cloth. Despite the expanding economy the gentle, rolling landscape remained essentially the same. Even today with its green fields, dry-stane dykes, blooming hedgerows, hidden coves and silver bays it would be instantly recognisable to Robert Burns as the place he came to spend the last years of his life.

Ellisland Farm

Ellisland Farm stands, slightly elevated, on the banks of the River Nith six miles north of the town of Dumfries. In the midst of this rich agricultural land it was Burns's lot to sign up for a farm with exhausted, undrained, unfertilised soil. In this he seems to have inherited his father's unerring instinct for a bad bargain. At £70 a year for the 170 acres it was indeed that. And it came minus a farmhouse. No doubt it was the location which took his eye, with views up and down the river and long walks on its tree-lined banks. For most of April and May of that year he travelled back and forth between Dumfriesshire and Mauchline visiting Jean and their one surviving child, a son, from the first pregnancy, while making preparations for the final move. His long pursuit of an excise appointment now came to fruition and in the month of April he began his training. At the back of his mind it was insurance in case the farming business failed. Or perhaps, even at this point in time, he was already considering abandoning farming even before he'd begun. In July he was issued with a commission, but it was September 1789 before he was given an appointment. With it came a salary of £50 per year.

In June, having made arrangements to lodge with a couple whose cottage lay on the Ellisland boundary, he moved down on a more permanent basis to begin work on the farm and plan and supervise the building of the farmhouse. He and Jean didn't set up home together until the end of the year. With the work on the farmhouse still far from complete he arranged to rent a nearby cottage, where they lived until the following summer when the house was finished. The house, which contained five rooms, has been altered and in part rebuilt since Burns's time, but the parlour and kitchen are still original. For the next three years, until November 1791, Burns lived there with Jean and their children combining the arduous life of working an unproductive farm with the duties of an excise officer.

Burns's friends during the Dumfriesshire years were many and varied. Robert Riddell of Glenriddell, who owned the estate known as Friars' Carse, which adjoined Ellisland to the north, wasted no time in getting to know the poet he'd heard so much about. A tall, handsome man with a booming laugh, sociable and well-educated, he had retired captain in the Scots Greys after the American War. Something of an antiquary, he was also an amateur musician and composer and shared a love of Scottish song with Burns. They became firm friends, Burns being a frequent visitor to the house. Riddell also gave his friend the key to the folly in the grounds, in order that he might have a place to work in privacy and peace. It stood in a copse of trees on the edge of the estate close to Ellisland and Burns suitably entitled his first composition 'Verses in Friars' Carse Hermitage', engraving the first lines on one of the windows of the hermitage with a diamond stylus, a habit he'd developed and which continued. He went on to produce a collection of letters and poems as a tribute to Riddell. But Friars' Carse was destined to hold bitter memories for Robert Burns and his 'Trusty Glenriddell'.

The house itself was originally a square tower owned by the monks of the Cistercian Order, which Robert Riddell had demolished and rebuilt into a comfortable, two storied home. This, in turn, was added to and altered by subsequent owners. The house today is red sandstone, Scots baronial style and run as a hotel. It stands on a picturesque bend in the river, surrounded by trees. The well-documented 'Whistle Contest' is said to have taken place on the night of 16 October, 1789 in what is now the dining-room. The tiny, ebony whistle immortalised in rhyme by Burns had come into the Riddell family generations earlier, when the family intermarried with the Lauries of Maxwelton. Sir Robert Laurie had prised it from a giant Dane, who had arrived in the country earlier in the century with the court of Prince George of Denmark. Previously unbeaten in the capitals of Europe he had to surrender his trophy to a Scot. At the beginning of the drinking joust the whistle is placed on the table and at the end of the evening whoever is capable of blowing the last blast is declared the winner. Now Robert Riddell gave Sir Robert Laurie's grandson and namesake the chance to claim back the whistle. The third participant in the contest was Sir Alexander Fergusson of Craigdarroch and it was he who carried away the trophy that evening, drinking in excess of eight bottles of claret. Two others acted as witnesses to declare the contest fair, while Burns sat quietly at a table by the window with paper and pen composing. He would brush it up and work on it later before presenting it to Riddell as a memento of the evening.

It was at Friars' Carse that Burns met the antiquarian Francis Grose. Researching for material for his volume 'Antiquities of Scotland' and looking for a supernatural tale, he convinced Burns to write one in exchange for the inclusion of a drawing of Alloway Kirkyard (see 'Tam o' Shanter'). And it was here two years later, at the end of 1791, that Maria Riddell, Robert's sister-in-law came into Burns's life. A tenant farmer on Riddell's estate William Lorimer of Kemys Hall, which lay downstream on the opposite side of the river from Ellisland, became a close friend. It was his beautiful daughter Jean of 'lint-white locks' fame who later became the poet's muse Chloris (see 'O Whistle and I'll come to you, my Lad').

Burns had a somewhat strained relationship with his landlord Patrick Miller, whose estate of Dalswinton stood on the other side of the river. Miller enjoyed basking in the glory of having Burns as a tenant and of being seen to be his benefactor, while at the same time treating the poet with a measure of condescension. And the farm he'd 'bestowed' on Burns was hardly an act of kindness, more the attitude 'we keeps a poet'.

In November 1791 Burns quit Ellisland. Managing to extricate himself from the lease, he moved his family into the town of Dumfries. The previous year had taken its toll on his health, a combination of work on the farm and the extensive travelling on horseback, which was required as part of his duty as an excise officer. Burns had been laying down plans for such an exit for the previous two years, always looking forward to the day when his vision of release from the yoke of the soil would harden into a reality. Promotion in 1790 had increased his salary to £70 a year plus the 'bonus' each officer was awarded, which constituted a monetary sum calculated as a percentage of any contraband seized. Despite his outbursts of Republican sympathy for the French Revolution, which were not in line with his masters the crown, Burns was a valued officer often commended and promoted.

In those days Dumfries was a bustling town. Robert Heron, writer and native Gallovidian described it:

> a considerable town, containing nearly 7000 inhabitants... a beautiful and advantageous situation... a sort of metropolis... a place of higher gaiety and elegance than any other town in Scotland of the same size

The town had its share of prosperous merchants alongside schools, libraries, banks, horse and cattle markets, two harbours serving a large bulk of shipping throughout the year, a printing house and a weekly newspaper, and by 1792 it could even boast its own theatre. For its size it had a disproportionate amount of 'society' with regular balls, routs and assemblies. These festivities were boosted even further during the winter months when many of the local gentry moved into their town houses. The Caledonian Hunt joined the local Dumfries and Galloway Hunt for races during the autumn months on Tinwald Downs, and even more colour was injected into the district when extra detachments of cavalry and infantry were billeted in this garrison town during the French Revolution. Burns loathed the strutting arrogance of the 'lobster-coated puppies' and made no secret of his contempt for them.

The Burns family initially lived in a small three-roomed flat on the first floor of a tenement at the beginning of Wee Vennel, a steep street running up at right angles from the Whitesands, which border the River Nith. In May 1793 they moved to a larger detached red sandstone house in Mill Hole Brae, now Burns Street, where the poet died three years later. With the physical and financial strain of farming finally behind him Burns could look forward to a brighter future. But it was not to be. His sins, as he lamented to Bob Ainslie, had caught up with him 'a monument of the vengeance laid up in store for the wicked'. In March of that year, Ann Park, a barmaid in the Globe Inn, his usual stopping-off place in Dumfries, produced his daughter. No fuss was made and Ann went off to her family in Leith to have the child. Jean had also produced their son William Nicol within a few days of Ann Park's daughter. Rab had indeed been up to his old tricks. Delayed in town some nights on excise business it was easier and safer during the winter months to stay overnight at the inn rather than try to return to Ellisland. At least that would be his excuse to Jean.

Now as they were barely settled in their cramped accommodation with two young boys and a baby of eight months Clarinda summoned him to Edinburgh reminding him of his duty to Jenny Clow, who was dying of consumption. Whether Jean knew about Jenny Clow's son or not, Burns must have been worried that although Jenny had earlier refused to allow him to take the boy she might now insist that he did. And it was always possible Ann Park could pop up out of the blue and demand he take their daughter. A year later he did bring their daughter back to Dumfries to be brought up by Jean, who took it all in her stride laughing 'Our Rab should have had twa wives'. A double-edged sword awaited him in Edinburgh, an angry Clarinda, but Clarinda all the same, and the dying mother of his son, who was entitled to insist he take their child. In the event she didn't. Around the time he returned to Dumfries to compose 'Ae Fond Kiss' that other amateur poetess, who was to fill the gap Clarinda left, was taking up residence in Friars' Carse.

Maria Riddell and her husband Walter had arrived from London with their baby daughter and were living with her brother-in-law and his wife Elizabeth, while searching for a house of their own. Attractive and flirtatious, Maria was nineteen years old and Burns thirty-three when they met. Well-educated and well-travelled, her father had twice been Governor of the Leeward Islands, where her family owned estates. She had produced her own volume about the flora and fauna of the islands and after pushing Burns for an introduction, the Edinburgh printer William Smellie published her book with the long-winded title *'Voyages to the Maderia and Leeward Caribbee Islands; with Sketches of the Natural History of These Islands'*. Initially she had expected to sell only a few copies, but Smellie liked it, saw the potential and printed five hundred.

The Riddells bought the estate Holm of Dalscairth on the outskirts of Dumfries on the Dalbeattie Road. Walter changed the name of the house from Goldielea to Woodley Park, as Woodley was Maria's maiden name. Burns was a frequent visitor to the house and Walter was often away. But like Nancy McLehose, because of the social divide, their relationship never ventured beyond the bounds of decorum. Until the night known as 'the Rape of the Sabine Women'. Up to that time Maria had filled a void in his life, both intellectually and emotionally. He was grief stricken to lose her. She was a capricious character, but with an underlying steely strength and a political astuteness. She knew how to woo and win whatever she wanted, but she was not without her detractors, mainly other women. In many ways she and Burns were very alike. Perhaps this is why her obituary for him rang so true. It took one to know one. It is apparent from her obituary that she had matured a great deal in the five years since she arrived in Dumfriesshire. She too had suffered from the estrangement. She revered Burns and stuck with him until the end and beyond, she did not sully his memory, though more than most she had felt the brunt of his anger delivered by the vicious side-swipes of his pen. When James Currie was putting together the first biography after the poet's death she kept him in line always in defence of Burns, the man and the poet. One request was met with the sharp rebuke 'What do you mean by desiring me to correct any thing of Burns? 'Tis asking me 'to paint the lily and add perfume to the violet'. In her astute and penetrating obituary, first printed in *The Dumfries Weekly Journal* she laid bare the war which constantly waged within him:

> Much indeed has been said of his inconstancy and caprice; but I am inclined to believe they originated less in a levity of sentiment, than from an extreme impetuosity of feeling which rendered him prompt to take umbrage; and his sensations of pique, where he fancied he had discovered the traces of unkindness, scorn or neglect, took their measure of asperity from the overflowing of the opposite sentiment which preceded them, and which seldom failed to regain its ascendency in his bosom, on the return of calmer reflection. He was candid and manly in the avowal of his errors and his avowal was reparation...too often unable to control the passions which proved a source of frequent errors and misfortunes to him, Burns made his own artless apology in language more impressive than all the argumentatory vindications in the world could do, in one of his own poems, where he delineates the gradual expansion of his mind to the lessons of the 'tutelary muse', who concludes an address to her pupil, almost unique for simplicity and beautiful poetry, with these lines:

> I saw thy pulse's madd'ning play
> Wild send thee Pleasure's devious way;
> Misled by Fancy's meteor ray,
> By passion driven;
> But yet the light that led astray,
> Was light from heaven!

> *(The Vision)*

The night, which ever after has been dubbed 'The Rape of the Sabine Women', began innocently enough. Robert and Elizabeth Riddell had invited a group of friends to dinner one evening towards the end of December in 1793. Maria's husband was abroad, but she was there, as were Burns, several other close friends and relatives and, so the story goes, several of the 'lobster-coated puppies'. The ladies withdrew after dinner leaving the men to their port, and it was then the plot was hatched to make a raid on the drawing-room as a prank on the ladies by pretending to act out the Roman myth of 'The Rape of the Sabine Women'. What exactly happened we don't know and whatever actually occurred has been scrambled in the mists of time. Each man was allotted a 'victim', Burns being given Maria. If what Burns said in the letter 'from the regions of Hell, amid the horrors of the damned', which he sent to Elizabeth Riddell as an apology, is true, and there is no reason to doubt it, some of the blame must lie with Robert Riddell in getting his guests very drunk. The 'charge' was led by Burns, who threw open the doors and rushed to grab Maria. Too late he realised he had been tricked, as the others waited by the doorway, paring their fingernails. The outrage of Elizabeth Riddell hit Burns full in the face and he was marched from the house. Some of the women pleaded for him, understanding what had happened, but to no avail. Elizabeth Riddell, society hostess and snob, saw an opportunity to remove the 'ploughman poet' from her husband's social circle. The family had a position to adopt. And the 'lobster-coated puppies', who trailed in Maria's wake, had their day.

A puzzle remains. Why would Robert Riddell treat such a good friend so badly? Why did he not step forward, smooth things over and own up to plying the men with too much port? If the others were determined to make a fool of Burns by either making sure he was drunk or goading him on to grab Maria, or both, why didn't he stop them? In this he broke all the bounds of hospitality, which his upbringing and rank would have led anyone to expect. But with an irate wife beside him and fairly puggled himself he acted the coward and took the easy way out. Elizabeth, on the other hand saw her chance; in one fell swoop she had Burns out of their lives, while at the same time quashing any gossip about Burns and Maria, which must have circulated freely in Dumfries at that time, whispers which she would feel soiled the family name. And as a bonus she now held the whiphand on Maria.

Four months later Robert Riddell was dead at the age of 38. Within a year both estates belonging to the Riddells had been sold and Elizabeth had moved to Edinburgh. Today, over two hundred years later the only reason the self-important Elizabeth Riddell and others of her ilk are given a mention is because of their connection with Robert Burns, otherwise they would be consigned to the dustbin of time.

A year was to pass before Burns and Maria were reunited. By then, with her husband in financial difficulties and having to remain in London, she chose to return to Dumfriesshire living alone with her two young daughters in a series of damp and draughty rented houses. Burns, meanwhile, had moved into the house in Mill Hole Brae to accommodate his growing family. During the early part of 1794 he tried again and again to contact Maria, but under Elizabeth's tutelage she steadfastly refused to forgive him. Rejected, his love turned to loathing, passion displaced, he produced a stream of vitriolic verse attacking her. And time didn't dim his distress. In the month of June 1794 he was playing the 'solitary hermit, in the solitary room' grumbling to Nancy McLehose about Maria, enclosing his latest invective about her. Little wonder she didn't reply. The message was he was sitting in a 'solitary inn,' but he wasn't sure if he was missing her or Maria! But he could be forgiven, for this was a technique he had used all his life: when he was suffering he assuaged the pain of the present by filtering it through intense joys from the past.

During the summer and autumn of 1794 Jean Lorimer came into Burns's life once more. After her brief marriage she had returned to her parents' home at Kemys Hall. Being in the company of this flaxen-haired beauty kept him distracted from the despair he felt over Maria. He wrote twenty-six songs as a tribute to her so it's fair to say he was taken with her. 'Platonic love' was how he described it in a letter to George Thomson, editor of *'Select Scottish Airs'*, insisting it was no more than that, 'Now don't put any of your squinting construction on this, or have any clishmaclaiver about it among your acquaintances'. There is no proof that it was more than friendship, but after January 1795, when he and Maria were reunited, there are no more poems for 'Chloris'.

No sooner was the breach healed with Maria than Burns managed to offend one of his oldest correspondents, Mrs Dunlop of Dunlop, an Ayrshire lady old enough to be his mother. She had latched on to him after reading the Kilmarnock edition of his poems, suggesting at the time that she become his 'literary critic'. While exercising rare tolerance at her suggestions for his work, not blind to the influence she could peddle on his behalf and ignoring the patronising manner she could adopt, there was genuine liking for this old lady. Whatever possessed him, knowing two of her daughters were married to exiled French royalists, to describe Louis XVI and Marie Antoinette as 'a perjured blockhead and an unprincipled prostitute' is anyone's guess. In subsequent letters he sent asking why he hadn't heard from her, he seemed oblivious to the hurt he might have caused. His witty flourish, as he no doubt saw it, nothing more than a stab in the air at the royalist cause, cost him her friendship. And try as he might he never heard from her again.

Apart from his poetic output and his compulsive letter writing during these Dumfriesshire years, Burns devoted his talents to writing, compiling and rearranging many Scottish songs, and without his dedication many lyrics and melodies would have been lost forever. From 1788 until 1792 he worked at this for James Johnson's *Scots Musical Museum* and continued from

1792 until his death in 1796 for George Thomson's' *'Select Scottish Airs'*. The debt we owe to him for this service is immeasurable, considering his other responsibilities, his failing health and that the work was unpaid.

The legacy of his childhood heart condition haunted Burns all his life. Since his death different doctors and biographers have come up with many contrasting theories as to what caused his death. Burns did not die from alcoholism, a popular misconception, which has ranged around in various forms. If we consider his poetical output, his large volume of correspondence, his work on Scottish songs and the hundreds of miles a week he travelled on horseback as an excise officer, it makes sense that Burns couldn't possibly have been an alcoholic – he simply didn't have the time! This theory of alcoholism is tied in with the documented fact that he was often affected by 'depressions'. Most people, having carried Burns's physical workload, running in tandem with his intellectual output, would certainly have been down from time to time, maybe even tired. Burns's 'depressions' were much more likely to have been caused by sheer mental and physical exhaustion. But the years at Mount Oliphant had damaged his heart in more ways than one and it is a testimony to his strength of character, rather than the introspective indulgence associated with alcoholism, that he soldiered on and achieved so much. He was afflicted with 'rheumatics' from time to time and this would not be at odds with the climatic conditions, especially working on the land and out in all weathers in the west coast of Scotland, the dampest part of the country. His 'shortness of breath' could be attributable to his heart condition or asthma or bronchitis or all three at varying times. Again in this part of Scotland these conditions are prevalent. His heart condition may have originated after a bout of undiagnosed rheumatic fever, it's a well-known consequence. This in turn would have been exacerbated by the heavy workload in his youth. It could also have been the reverse, the heavy workload causing such a deleterious effect on his health he succumbed to infection. Now, in this last year of his life, he was suffering from joint pains, believed to be rheumatism. His doctors were culpable in hastening his death by sending him to the spa at the Brow Well, south of Dumfries, to drink the waters and immerse himself in the icy Solway. His illness was labelled with the ludicrous term 'flying gout'. It was more likely he was in the final stages of rheumatoid arthritis and this combined with a heart complaint, would explain his severe pain. The last thing he needed was to be plunged into icy cold water.

Maria Riddell saw Burns for the final time early in July. Staying at Lochmaben for a change of air as her own health was poor, she sent her carriage to collect him:

> I was struck with his appearance on entering the room. The stamp of death was imprinted on his features. He seemed already touching the brink of eternity. His first salutation was: 'Well, madam, have you any commands for the other world?'

They met again on the following day, 6 July. The last memory she had of him was 'as he stood at the door of a miserable cottage by the sea'. Burns was in no doubt he was dying. One sunny afternoon, while staying at the Brow Well he visited Rev. Craig and his family at Ruthwell. Concerned about his frail condition and realising the sun was blinding the poet and might be too bright for him, Agnes Craig, the minister's daughter rose to close the blinds only to hear Burns's plea: 'Thank you, my dear, for your kind attention; but oh, let him shine: he will not shine long for me!' Robert Burns died on 21 July 1796, aged 37, but the shock which triggered his final decline was the death of his daughter Elizabeth in September 1795. His love for his children was sacrosanct and for a time he was inconsolable. During the following winter his health seesawed up and down, but although struggling, he was still working and composing in the last few months of his life. By then he was seriously worried about his finances should his pay be reduced and what would be his family's future if he died.

Acute shortages of food during the winter had caused hardship all over the country and during February and March there were riots in the streets of Dumfries. In the event his pay was reduced and, panic-stricken, he asked friends to repay money he had loaned and begged others for financial assistance to pay small accounts. His finances were not as dire as he believed, his health was so bad he simply couldn't think straight.

Burns's fears for Jean and the children proved unfounded, due to the unstinting efforts of his friends, Alexander Cunningham and John Syme. They collected a substantial sum of money through public subscription and from the sales of his work to ensure a comfortable and secure lifestyle for the family. Burns was buried on 25 July 1796 in St Michael's Churchyard, Dumfries. Thousands lined the street of the town to pay their last respects. Jean, absent from the funeral as she was giving birth to their youngest child, outlived him by 38 years, dying in 1834 at the age of 67. Jean Armour was married to Burns for only eight years. In that time she bore his children and took in others he'd produced elsewhere. She ran their home and nurtured their family. Very little is known about her, always painted as a saint, nonetheless she was a flesh-and-blood woman with her own wants and desires, tempers and frustrations. That Robert Burns loved her there can be no doubt; she created the home and hearth where he was husband and father and these things were vital to his existence. But there was always that other Robert Burns, who yearned for the wider world, where he roamed wild and free belonging to no one.

There was one love in Burns's life that no earthly being could surpass or even come close to, and that was the Muse. And Burns didn't find the Muse, she came for him and she gave him immortality. She reigned in his passions and frustrations, made substance of them, honed them into something beautiful and everlasting, so that 200 years later Burns still draws you in, his powers of seduction undiminished.

THE HISTORY OF
THE BURNS SUPPER

The tradition of the Burns Supper in recognition and celebration of the poet's life and work began in the early years after his death. The first recorded supper occurred in Ayrshire in the summer of 1801, although others are believed to have taken place earlier. Held in Burns Cottage in Alloway (then an inn), the party consisted of nine of Burns's closest friends, including Robert Aiken, the eloquent lawyer, and John Ballantine, the provost of Ayr. The speech was given by the Reverend Hamilton Paul and, even here at the first recorded dinner, haggis was served. It was decided at this meeting that the following year's gathering should take place on the poet's birthday in January and because of a mistake in Currie's biography of Burns (corrected some years later) this was thought to be 29 January. Over the next ten years the date for the dinners shifted between winter and summer, but eventually, due to pressure of work in the farming community during the summer months, it was decided that January was the most suitable time.

It is difficult to date when this steadily growing circle actually became the Alloway Burns Club, but by the end of the first decade of the 19th century they were certainly known as such. During the early years other Burns clubs sprang up in Greenock, Paisley and Kilmarnock and, helped by increasing press coverage, word of these events soon spread until the original concept of a dinner commemorating the poet was taken up by groups of individuals and clubs, who added a Burns Supper to their yearly programme. By 1830 these gatherings were widespread, not just in Ayrshire and Dumfriesshire, where Burns had lived, but all over the country. These clubs, although run on an informal basis, were the forerunners of the official Burns clubs of today. The parent body of this worldwide association is the Burns Federation, based in Kilmarnock, which at present lists 300-400 affiliated clubs and between 200 and 300 individuals as active federation members.

There is an important distinction between a Burns Supper and the Burns Anniversary Dinner given by Burns clubs. Club Anniversary Dinners have the early format of speeches, music and song, 'The Immortal Memory' being the high point of an evening dedicated to Burns's life and work. Burns Suppers follow this style, but some are on a looser framework and some end the evening with a dance. Needless to say, traditionalists frown on this addition to the event, but it is certainly one way of introducing younger generations to a Burns Supper and the poet's work.

There are also those who disapprove of having women at a Burns Supper, even today some clubs will not allow it, which seems at odds with Burns's own life and ignores the fact that a lady (Primrose Kennedy of Drumellan) attended the first dinner in Alloway. The 'lasses', however, have occasionally got their own back. In 1920, in Shotts in Lanarkshire, the first all ladies' club was founded; there was in fact quite a spate of these all ladies' clubs in the district at that time. The Burns Federation itself has, to date, had four women presidents. The first, in 1970, was Jane Burgoyne, an Edinburgh teacher.

The 'Toast to the Lasses' has also undergone a change from earlier days. Originally it was a thank you to the ladies for supplying the food for the evening, by way of a salute to them for their kindness. It didn't take the form it does now, whereby the 'lasses' are lambasted for their failings, before being praised for their attributes. In the earlier speeches, too, the only ladies mentioned were those in Burns's life. At 'Bachelor' Suppers, a gentleman delivers 'The Reply' on behalf of the 'lasses'.

The most atmospheric of all Burns Suppers is said to take place in the Globe Inn in Dumfries. A regular haunt of the poet, so strong is the memory of him that, to quote Mr Ogilvie, past president of the Dumfries Burns Club, 'should the spirit of Burns appear at the table, no one would be surprised'. Certainly the inn has the feeling that time has passed it by, particularly in a room upstairs where Burns scratched some lines on the window and nothing feels as if it has changed for centuries. The Dumfries Burns Club itself was not founded until 1820, although the previous year's celebrations to mark the poet's birthday had been held at the inn.

It was during the earlier dinner in 1819 that the decision was taken to order, from Spode, a porcelain punch bowl to be used on all future occasions. It came with a silver ladle, mugs and three dozen glasses. Decorated with Burns's portrait surrounded by depictions of the important places in his life, the centre of the bowl has a painting of the Mausoleum in Dumfries; thistles, leaves and fruit are intertwined throughout and on the bottom rim there are replicas of the signatures of the group of his friends who commissioned the bowl. It can be seen today along with other Burns memorabilia in the Robert Burns Centre in Dumfries.

The Globe Inn, Dumfries

The Burns Supper exists as a celebration of the art and endeavour of the poet. But the underlying objective and ultimately the best test of a successful evening is how many of the guests have their love of Burns rekindled and how many others go home determined to read him for the first time. The event should not be just a celebration, with all the pleasure that this entails, it should also act as a reaffirmation of the humanitarian values enshrined in his work.

THE BASIC ELEMENTS OF A BURNS SUPPER

THE ORDER OF EVENTS

Whether a Burns Supper is organised by a Burns Club, any other club or a group of friends, the basic format is the same. After the Chairman for the evening has welcomed the company, a recitation of 'The Selkirk Grace' follows. Dinner is served, including the piping-in of the haggis and then a rendering of Burns's 'Address to the Haggis'. After the meal is finished, the principal speaker is called upon to deliver the main speech of the evening 'The Immortal Memory'. This is followed by a short appreciation of his efforts and the two other compulsory speeches, 'The Toast to the Lasses' and 'The Reply'. Other speeches can be included: the Ayr Burns Club always has a toast to 'Auld Ayr'. Songs and recitations follow the speeches and the evening is brought to a close by the singing of 'Auld Lang Syne'.

The evening can thus be broken up into three main sections: the Dinner, the Speeches, and the Songs and Recitations.

THE DINNER

1 The Chairman welcomes the company.
2 The clergyman recites 'The Selkirk Grace'.
3 Dinner is served including the piping-in of the haggis
   and a rendering of Burns's 'To a Haggis'.
4 The Chairman proposes 'The Loyal Toast'.

5   The club Secretary makes any announcements about future events and plans.

THE SPEECHES

1   The principal speaker is called upon to deliver 'The Immortal Memory'.
2   A short speech in appreciation of his efforts is given.
3   'The Toast to the Lasses' is proposed by a gentleman speaker.
4   'The Reply' from a lady speaker follows.
5   Other speeches and toasts can now be added.

THE SONGS AND RECITATIONS

1   Various songs and recitations of Burns's work.
2   The evening ends with the company singing 'Auld Lang Syne'.

As a guideline the proceedings should last from 6.30 pm until 11.00 pm.

HOW TO ORGANISE
A BURNS SUPPER

WHERE TO BEGIN

When considering arranging a Burns Supper, first contact your local Burns Club or the Burns Federation in Kilmarnock for help. Your local club will be able to give advice, perhaps suggest speakers and tell you of other Burns Suppers in the area, which might clash with the evening you have chosen.

THE DATE

A Burns Supper does not have to take place on 25 January, it can be given any time in the weeks preceding or following the anniversary of the poet's birth. It will also be easier to find good speakers if you are prepared to move further away from the actual date.

THE ORGANISER

The first task in front of anyone planning a Burns Supper is to delegate an organiser, preferably with a few able helpers. In the official Burns clubs the duty of organiser usually falls to the Secretary, who can enlist the aid of two or three committee members. Other clubs deciding to add a Burns Supper to their diary of events should follow the same guidelines. Having a Burns Supper at home can be fun, more relaxed and less nerve-racking, especially if you've been asked to give a speech or recitation. Get friends to give the speeches, slay the haggis, sing the songs, play the pipes or the fiddle and bring different courses for the meal.

THE CHAIRMAN

After the organiser is chosen, a Chairman should be appointed for the evening. Normally, but not necessarily, this role falls to the club President. Whoever takes on the task should be adept at, and have experience of, guiding an evening from the introductory speech through to the final farewell. It requires a commanding, but genial host, preferably someone with a love of Burns, who can keep control of the arrangements, especially the timing, introduce the performers and speakers and at the beginning be able to set a warm, inspiring tone for the evening ahead.

The essential ingredients for the festivities are as follows:

1. A clergyman to deliver 'The Selkirk Grace'.
2. A piper to pipe in the haggis or perhaps a fiddler (it has been done).
3. A speaker for the principal speech of the evening 'The Immortal Memory'.
4. A speaker for 'The Toast to the Lasses'.
5. A lady to deliver 'The Reply'.
6. Two or three speakers to deliver recitations of Burns's poems.
7. A male and female vocalist for Burns's songs.
8. An accompanist for the vocalists, pianist or fiddler or both.

THE HOTEL

If you do decide to hold a supper begin arrangements as early as possible. It is never too early to book the hotel, speakers, singers, accompanists and the piper. Inspect a few hotels; most will have had some experience of catering for a Burns Supper, whether large or small scale. Ask for a quotation from each, for the cost of the function suite, including a separate reception room for the top table guests, dinner and any drinks served as part of the proceedings. Most good hotels will be able to offer various menus for a Burns Supper and be prepared to negotiate prices. Haggis does not have to be the main course, it can be served as a replacement for the traditional fish course. Details you will need for the manager are: the approximate length of the evening (is there to be a dance after the dinner and speeches?), how formal the style, and a rough idea of numbers. At this stage you should also discuss various dates available at the hotels before contacting the speakers.

SPEAKERS

The principal speech is 'The Immortal Memory' and whoever delivers this is largely responsible for the success of the evening. Contact your local Burns Club or the Burns Federation about finding a good speaker (the best are often booked years ahead) and ask friends and colleagues from other clubs and societies to recommend their past successes. Once a speaker has been decided upon, after a meeting to assess his talents or better still having listened to him speak, the club Secretary should then write inviting him to speak, remembering the greater his reputation the sooner you will have to try. If an agreement is reached and a date fixed, you should, even at this early stage, give him a brief résumé of your club, its history and an outline of the tone, style and hopes you have for your dinner. The other speakers, who deliver 'The Toast to the Lasses' and 'The Reply' are invited to take part some six to eight months before the event. In many Burns clubs these two speakers can be found amongst the members. At a later date it's a good idea to put the speakers in touch with one another to avoid any duplication of material. It should be agreed at an early stage just how long each speech will last. 'The Immortal Memory' should last approximately twenty to thirty minutes and the other two speeches a maximum of ten minutes each. It is customary that an invitation to speak includes a supper invitation for the speaker's partner.

THE CLERGYMAN, SINGERS, ACCOMPANISTS, READERS AND THE PIPER

The clergyman, singers, accompanists, readers and the piper are also invited guests at the feast. They should be contacted as soon as possible and their part in the evening's entertainment explained. Most will have experience of Burns Suppers and will know exactly what is expected of them.

FEES

The question of fees for speakers and performers rarely arises within Burns club circles, only occasional travelling expenses being necessary. However, professional speakers and performers would be paid for their services.

FOLLOW-UP PLANS

Once the arrangements for speakers, performers and hotel have been agreed and confirmed in writing, they should be contacted again in early December to remind them of their commitments. By this time whoever is to deliver 'The Immortal Memory' will have a basic speech plan prepared. At this juncture the Secretary, Chairman and a few committee members from the club should meet the speaker for a final briefing. This should be an opportunity for all views to be aired and any misunderstandings that might have occurred to be cleared up. The speaker should be reminded of the club's hopes for the evening, given details of the level of formality, the length of the proceedings, how long he is expected to speak, whether there will be any distinguished guests and the total number expected to attend. Moreover, this is the time to ask someone from the club to prepare an alternative speech, should be speaker become ill or be unable to attend at the last minute.

DRESS

Everyone involved in the evening should be advised about dress. At a Burns Club Anniversary Dinner, guests at the top table wear evening dress, some Highland dress, while the other guests dress informally. This is a good rule to follow, but there is nothing to prevent the other guests wearing evening dress if they choose and at some large formal dinners it is compulsory for all. It is often requested that everyone wear an item of tartan.

INVITATIONS, TICKETS, PROGRAMMES

Invitations to the dinner are issued by the club Secretary. Apart from the speakers and performers, local dignitaries are usually included. Within the Burns club circle this honour would also be extended to members, friends and visitors and there is no maximum or minimum number for a Burns Supper. Before working out a ticket price you must take all the expenses into consideration (ie the cost of the dinner plus the hiring of the function suite, any expenses incurred by speakers or performers, printer's costs, postage and any miscellaneous outgoings). Tickets and programmes should be printed, but perhaps the costs could be reduced if you have a printer within the club or society. Alternatively, using a computer and good quality card you could print your own. The programme includes the menu, or 'bill of fare' as it is called and a list of the speeches, speakers and performers. A programme for each guest, to keep as a memento of the occasion, should be displayed on the table. A typical evening's programme of the Ayr Burns Club, courtesy of the Secretary, Mrs Martha McKellar is shown overleaf.

AYR BURNS CLUB FEDERATION NO. 275

Bill o' Fare

'Some hae meat and canna eat
And some wad eat that want it:
But we hae meat and we can eat,
And sae the Lord be thankit.'

Cock-a-Leekie

Haggis,
warm, reekin, rich wi'
Champit Tatties, Bashed Neeps

Address to the Haggis
Mr A. McPherson

Steak Pie

Tipsy Laird

A Tassie o' Coffee

TOAST LIST

Grace . . . . Rev. D. Ness

The Queen . . . . The Chairman

Greetings from Kindred Clubs . . . .   Hon. Secretary

THE IMMORTAL MEMORY
Mr Tom Raffel

Song . . . . Miss Ann Maclachlan

Auld Ayr . . . . Mr Philip Craig

Reading . . . . Mrs Jeanette Service

Reply . . . . Provost Daniel McNeill

Song . . . . Mr David Boyd

Reading . . . . Mrs Jeanette Service

The Lassies . . . . Rev. David Ness

Song . . . . Miss Ann Maclachlan

Reply . . . . Rev. Effie Campbell

Song . . . . Mr David Boyd

Vote of Thanks . . . . Mrs Roma Ferguson

Accompanist . . . . Mrs Jean Kean

Piper . . . . Mr John Paton

SEATING PLANS

The top-table party consists of the Chairman, the speakers, the minister, other specially invited guests and local dignitaries, along with their respective partners. They gather in a separate reception room for drinks before the evening begins. A seating plan should be on display in this room as the party must be arranged in order before leaving to be piped into the main dining-room.

TOP TABLE PLAN

1 Invited guest

2 Speaker's partner

3 Speaker – 'The Toast to the Lasses'

4 Speaker's partner

5 Speaker – 'The Immortal Memory'

6 The Chairman

7 Speaker's partner

8 The Minister

9 Speaker – 'The Reply'

10 Club Secretary

11 Speaker's partner

12 Invited guest

It is the job of the Secretary to ensure that the party is formed into a procession and arrives at the table in the order shown on the plan. Decisions on the table placings are taken by the Secretary and Chairman together. There is no set order to be followed, it is merely a matter of personal choice and discretion. The only exception to this is that the proposer of 'The Immortal Memory' sits on the Chairman's right-hand side. A table plan is also needed for all the other guests at the Supper, ensuring the company is well mixed, with committee members and any other specially invited guests spread throughout. There will always be last-minute alterations in the seating plan due to illness or cancellations. Consult the hotel manager and his staff, they will know best how to rearrange the numbers and tables.

THE FINAL ARRANGEMENTS

A week before the event visit the hotel once more and discuss with the manager any details that either of you may have overlooked. This will give you another chance to see the function suite (it may not be quite as you remember), double check the table layout, menu and drinks facilities and seating arrangements, making sure that there is space for the piper to reach the top table (the piper and procession will move clockwise round the room to the seats). On the day itself visit the hotel to inspect the tables, make any change of seating and deliver the programmes. In the evening, once the guests have arrived and had drinks, the Secretary and a few committee members can ensure everyone finds their allotted seat on the plan.

THE PRESS

A short press release should be sent to the local newspaper, with notes on speakers and performers. If the event is not covered by a journalist (this can be averted by sending an invitation to the local newspaper editor), details about the evening can be delivered, faxed or e-mailed the following day.

THE DINNER

> Some hae meat and canna eat
> And some wad eat that want it:
> But we hae meat and we can eat,
> And sae the Lord be thankit.
> *(The Selkirk Grace)*

RECITATION OF 'THE SELKIRK GRACE'

Once the company are in their places the piper proceeds to lead in the top-table guests. The assembly is signalled to stand and begins a handclap, while the procession moves clockwise around the room to their seats. As soon as everyone is seated, the Chairman will rise to make a short speech of welcome. This lasts only a few minutes and sets a convivial tone for the evening ahead. In addition to the printed programme he will have a more detailed list of speakers and performers and, during the rest of the evening, before introducing each speaker, he will deliver a short preamble on his or her background, including anything relevant to Burns and his work. After the welcome, grace is said, either by a clergyman or the Chairman himself. 'The Selkirk Grace' is normally chosen and the story behind its association with Burns is an interesting one.

In the summer of 1793 Burns and his friend John Syme set off on a tour of Galloway, staying for a few nights in the Selkirk Arms Hotel in Kirkcudbright. A plaque in the hotel claims that 'The Selkirk Grace' was composed there during this visit, but in actual fact it was recited by Burns at the home of the Earl of Selkirk on St Mary's Isle, an outshoot of land running from the town of Kirkcudbright into the Solway Firth. A day which had started out with Burns in a bad mood, a rainstorm having ruined his best pair of leather boots, finished happily at the Earl's dinner table, Burns at his scintillating best, impressing his host and charming the other guests. Burns and Syme arrived when the meal was well under way, but he was invited to say a grace before the next course. He adapted the old Scots grace, which had previously been known as the 'Galloway Grace' or the 'Covenanter's Grace', which thereafter became known as 'The Selkirk Grace'. Another guest of the Earl's that evening was Pietro Urbani, the Italian singer and composer, and it seems that he and Burns discussed the lyrics and tune for 'Scots Wha Hae', which Burns was working on at the time.

Dinner is then served. Cock-a-leekie soup is the standard first course. This is followed by the haggis with champit tatties and bashed neeps (mashed potatoes and mashed turnip). Today haggis is synonymous with Burns Night. No longer regularly made in Scottish households, as it was in the poet's lifetime, it has assumed a kind of magical significance on 25 January and is itself almost an honorary guest at the feast. The 'slaying' of the haggis is a vital part of the evening's ritual, probably more famous than many of the other ingredients of the Burns Supper.

THE HAGGIS CEREMONY

The haggis ceremony begins when the Chairman is signalled from the kitchen that all is ready. He asks the company to stand to receive the haggis and the piper or fiddler then leads in the chef carrying the haggis aloft, followed by a third person with two bottles of whisky. They march around the room to the top table, while the guests perform a slow handclap. The platter is placed on the table in front of the Chairman, who invites the chef and piper to join him in a glass of whisky to toast the haggis. Together they raise their glasses in the Gaelic toast *Slainte mhath* (pronounced 'slan-je-va') – your good health. The chef and piper then leave the proceedings (the piper rejoining his table) and the company take their seats. The Chairman or an invited guest then recites 'To a Haggis'.

To a Haggis

Fair fa' your honest, sonsie face	*good luck to – jolly*
Great Chieftain o' the Puddin-race!	
Aboon them a' ye tak your place,	*above*
Painch, tripe, or thairm:	*paunch – intestines*
Weel are ye wordy o' a grace	*worthy*
As lang's my arm.	
The groaning trencher there ye fill,	
Your hurdies like a distant hill,	*buttocks*
Your pin wad help to mend a mill	*would*
In time o' need,	
While thro' your pores the dews distil	
Like amber bead.	
His knife see Rustic-labour dight,	*clean, wipe*
An' cut you up wi' ready sleight,	
Trenching your gushing entrails bright	
Like onie ditch;	*any*
And then, O what a glorious sight,	
Warm-reekin, rich!	*steaming*

Then, horn for horn they stretch an' strive,	*horn – spoon*
Deil tak the hindmost, on they drive,	*last*
Till a' their weel-swall'd kytes belyve	*swelled stomachs*
	by-and-by
Are bent like drums;	
Then auld Guidman, maist like to rive,	*almost – burst*
'Bethankit' hums.	*murmurs 'God be thanked'*

Is there that owre his French *ragout*,	*over*
Or *olio* that wad staw a sow,	*would surfeit*
O *fricassee* wad mak her spew	
Wi' perfect sconner,	*disgust*
Looks down wi' sneering, scornfu' view	
On sic a dinner?	

Poor devil! see him ower his trash,	
As feckless as a wither'd rash,	*feeble – rush*
His spindle shank a guid whip-lash,	*thin leg – good*
His nieve a nit;	*clost fist – nut*
Thro' bluidy flood or field to dash,	*bloody*
O how unfit!	

But mark the Rustic, haggis-fed,	
The trembling earth resounds his tread;	
Clap in his walie nieve a blade,	*large fist*
He'll mak it whissle;	*whistle*
An' legs, an' arms, an' heads will sned	*lop off*
Like taps o' thrissle.	*tops of thistles*

Ye Pow'rs wha mak mankind your care
And dish them out their bill o' fare,

Auld Scotland wants nae skinking ware	*thin stuff*
That jaups in luggies;	*splashes in bowls*
But if ye wish her gratefu' prayer,	
Gie her a Haggis!	*Give*

The poem can be read, but the spectacle looks and sounds better if the words are memorised and delivered with enthusiasm. A knife should already be to hand on the table and as the speaker reaches the line, 'An' cut you up wi' ready sleight', he slits open the haggis. If the haggis has been cooked in the traditional manner, it will be encased in animal intestine and as such is difficult to cut. To avoid any embarrassment on the part of the speaker, ensure that a sharp-pointed knife is supplied. There are many different ways to perform this operation, but bear in mind that the object of the exercise is to be able to spoon out the contents on to the waiting plates. It is customary to applaud when the speaker finishes the address and at some Burns Suppers the company stands to toast the haggis with a glass of whisky. Although frowned upon by purists, in some clubs and at many Burns Suppers today, haggis is no longer the main course. Instead it appears on the menu in place of the fish course. Beef or turkey are popular main-course choices, and are especially welcomed by those who have not quite attained the superlative palate of the seasoned haggis connoisseur. Tipsy Laird, or sherry trifle as it is better known, is one of the most favoured puddings, but others are equally acceptable. A Scottish cheese served with oatcakes follows or coffee can be served directly after the pudding.

'THE LOYAL TOAST'

Once dinner is over, this section of the evening is brought to a close by the Chairman asking the company to stand and drink a toast to the health of the monarch.

CLUB ANNOUNCEMENTS

In Burns clubs this is the time for the Secretary to read out any messages of goodwill from other clubs and make announcements about club events or future plans.

BILL O' FARE

COCK-A-LEEKIE SOUP

Ingredients:

1 boiling fowl (roughly 3 lbs/1.4 kg)
giblets
4 pt/2 L water
6 leeks, cleaned and sliced

1 bouquet garni
8 prunes (soaked overnight)
salt and pepper

METHOD
Put the fowl and giblets into a large pan and cover with water. Add leeks, bouquet garni and seasonings. Bring to the boil, skim the surface, cover and simmer for 2 hours or until the bird is tender. Remove the fowl, discard giblets and bouquet garni, skim any fat from the surface. Add prunes, cook for a further 30 minutes, check seasonings and serve. The chicken can be used as a separate course or served cold later.
(Serves 6 – 8)

THE HAGGIS

Most haggis eaten nowadays is commercially prepared, whereas in the past it was produced at home from everyday cheap cuts of meat combined with oatmeal, onion, seasonings and beef suet, the whole minced and sewn up in a sheep's stomach before being boiled for three hours. The traditional recipe is as follows.

Ingredients:

1 sheep's stomach bag	8 oz/227 g oatmeal (pinhead)
2 onions	stock or gravy
1 sheep's pluck (heart, lights and liver)	1 teaspoon ground black pepper
1 tablespoon salt	8 oz/227 g beef suet

METHOD
Clean the stomach bag by washing thoroughly, turn inside out, scald and scrape with a knife. Soak overnight in cold salted water. Wash the pluck well, place in a large saucepan of cold water and bring to the boil. Hang the windpipe over the side of the pan. Boil for two hours, remove (reserve liquid) and mince the heart and lights and grate the liver. Put all the meat

into a bowl, add onions (finely chopped), oatmeal (toasted in the oven), suet and seasonings. Mix and add enough of the cooking liquid or fresh stock to moisten the mixture well. Fill the stomach bag slightly over half full and sew it up with strong thread. Prick the skin in a few places to prevent it bursting during cooking. Sit the haggis on a metal plate in a saucepan of boiling water (enough to cover the haggis) and boil for three hours, without lid. Keep adding boiling water to keep haggis covered. Serve with mashed potatoes and mashed turnip.

Ready-made haggis from butchers and supermarkets can be reheated (since it is already cooked) in one of two ways. Either place in a casserole with a little water in a moderate oven or heat in a good amount of water in a pot on top of the stove. Both methods require cooking for between half and three quarters of an hour per lb (500g) and the haggis should always be wrapped in foil. It should be thoroughly heated and served as hot as possible, with mashed turnip and potatoes.

For some, haggis is an acquired taste, but nevertheless it is eaten regularly in many parts of the world (including Scotland), not just at Burns Suppers or on St Andrews Night, but as a customary part of the diet. Today haggis consumption is actually increasing and for those who no longer eat meat, some butchers now produce a vegetarian alternative. Butchers can supply haggis in either the natural skin or a plastic covering; the only benefit to be gained from the artificial one, if ordering by post, is that it keeps better. Size is variable: from as small as 12 oz/340 g up to 4 lb/1.8 kg.

TYPSY LAIRD (SHERRY TRIFLE)

Ingredients:

1 Victoria sponge cake
(cut into slices)
12 oz/340 g raspberry jam
1 wine glass of sherry
2 tablespoons brandy or if
preferred Drambuie

Homemade egg custard
(see below)
12 oz/340 g raspberries
2 bananas (optional)
1/2 pt/300 ml double cream
1 tablespoon caster sugar
toasted almonds

CUSTARD

Ingredients:

8 fl oz /250 ml milk
5 fl oz /150 ml double cream
2 egg yolks

1 oz /28 g castor sugar
few drops vanilla essence

METHOD

Place the sponge in the base of a large glass bowl and spread with the raspberry jam. Mix the sherry and brandy and sprinkle evenly over the sponge allowing it to soak in. Next add a layer of raspberries and sliced bananas.

To make the custard, whisk together the egg yolks, sugar and vanilla essence until pale and creamy. Heat the milk and cream together in a saucepan until boiling point then stir into the egg mixture. Once it is well blended, return to the pan and stir continuously over a low heat until the custard thickens. Pour into a dish and allow to cool. When quite cool, pour the custard over the layer of fruit, spreading evenly. Next whip the double cream, add sugar to sweeten and spoon on top of custard. Decorate with toasted almonds.

Serves 6 – 8

CHEESES

Any Scottish cheese is suitable for Burns Night. Some of the better known are Orkney Cheddar, Crowdie, and Islay Dunlop.

THE IMMORTAL MEMORY SPEECH

WHERE TO BEGIN

After dinner there is a break in the proceedings for approximately 15 minutes. The company then return to their seats and the atmosphere is prepared for the second part of the evening, sometimes by a song or a tune on the fiddle. This paves the way for the Chairman to introduce the principal speaker and the high point of the evening: 'The Immortal Memory' speech. The Chairman should give a brief résumé of the speaker's life and interests, particularly those points associated with Burns and his work; any books written, speeches made or simply his knowledge and love of Burns.

There are many different types of 'Immortal Memory' speech, from the lighthearted to the literary, but they all have one thing in common – they should be a combination of warmth, reflection and wit.

If you're a complete novice and you've been asked to deliver a speech, concentrate on what you would really like to say as much as what you feel you should say.

Why has 'Auld Lang Syne' been adopted as an international anthem? Look at the universal nature of Burns's work. It has captured hearts and minds worldwide for over 200 years. Why?

The best place to start, even if you're not a newcomer to his work, is to get hold of a copy of the poems and songs. I defy you not to be swept up by their passion and sentiment, and it's not difficult, while reading them, to imagine him composing as he worked in the fields and later, when the house was quiet, sitting by candlelight writing and refining them. In many of the poems, what comes through is the humanity of the man, his depiction of those moments in all our lives when we come to realise what is and what is not important. Not what we can live with, but what we can't live without. Popular opinion has Burns's name forever marked down as synonymous with wine, women and song, but there was more to the man than that.

You could dip into some of the biographies for ideas (see suggestions at the back of the book), and there are many books and references on Ayrshire and Dumfriesshire of the period with information on Burns.

Burns as a Scotsman is an important part of the speech, especially to those expatriate Scots at dinners abroad, but avoid being too narrowly nationalistic and try to introduce a universal feel to the speech.

> Then let us pray that come it may, –
> As come it will for a' that –
> That Sense and Worth, o'er a' the earth,
> May bear the gree, and a' that.   *supremacy*
> For a' that, and a' that,
> It's comin' yet for a' that,

THE IMMORTAL MEMORY SPEECH

> That Man to Man, the world o'er,
> Shall brothers be for a' that!
>
> *(A Man's a Man for a' That)*

Like the sentiments in 'Auld Lang Syne' these suppers have continued down through the years. They help to keep the spirit of Burns alive and tonight you are a link in that chain. 'Kindred Clubs' is one of the toasts at the supper, but kindred spirits best describes those who feel a harmony with Burns and his beliefs.

In the following pages you will find a choice of themes for 'The Immortal Memory' speech. Each examines a certain feature of Burns's life and work. You could begin by using a text to emphasise this feature, developing your speech around it, using quotes from Burns and others. You can mention other poets and writers and what they owe to Burns. You should take into consideration the club or gathering you are addressing and what they expect from the speech. Finish by summing up, perhaps giving a new focus on the theme.

Try out your speech on one or two friends before the evening. Ask them to time it for you, make suggestions and give constructive criticism. Practise breathing and timing, which will build your confidence. Most inexperienced speakers begin too quickly, desperate, as they see it, to get the agony over as soon as possible. A natural calmness does take over once the speaker realises that he or she can't continue at breakneck speed, and on the run down towards the end most speakers, no matter how inexperienced, are sorry that it's finished.

At the end of the speech you should ask the company to rise and drink a toast to 'The Immortal Memory of Robert Burns'.

SUGGESTED THEMES FOR
'THE IMMORTAL MEMORY' SPEECH

BURNS'S LIFE

Anyone being asked to deliver 'The Immortal Memory' for the first time automatically thinks of the speech in terms of Burns's life. You will see from the following selection of topics that a detailed examination of Burns's life from birth to death is not essential. Rather, to keep your audience's attention and hopefully encourage their interest in Burns, try to look at the circumstances of his life from an unusual angle. It could, for example, be split into two stages: that is, after Edinburgh and at the end of his days in Dumfries. You could also ponder on what might have been Burns's thoughts at these times.

Although written years earlier, the last two verses of 'To a Mouse' sum up what must have been his feelings as he returned to the farmer's life after the heady days and raised hopes of Edinburgh:

> But Mousie, thou art no thy lane,   *not alone*
> In proving foresight may be vain:
> The best-laid schemes o' Mice an' Men
> Gang aft a-gley,   *go often wrong*
> An' lea'e us nought but grief and pain,   *leave*
> For promis'd joy.

> Still thou art blest, compar'd wi' me!
> The present only toucheth thee:
> But, Och! I backward cast my e'e,
> On prospects drear!

> An' forward, tho' I canna see,
> I guess an' fear!

As a further help, a selection of quotations is given at the back of the book.

Introduction – *The Ayrshire background*

Until the Kilmarnock edition of his poems was published and he started on the road to fame, but sadly not fortune, Robert Burns led a largely isolated life in Ayrshire. There, he 'first committed the sin of ryhme' at the age of 15 and there also, some ten years later, he began composing the works which made his reputation and ensured his place in literary history. You could at this point give a short description of the working conditions of an Ayrshire farmer at that time, emphasising Burns's great achievements both physical and literary. But even in difficult days, Burns always found cause to smile, whether in mirth at his fellow man, in companionship with the animals who shared his burdens, or simply at the sheer joy of being alive.

> The honest heart that's free frae a'
> Intended fraud or guile,
> However Fortune kick the ba',   *ball*
> Has ay some cause to smile;
>
> *(Epistle to Davie)*

Development – *After Edinburgh*

By the end of 1786 the Ayrshire farmer had become the toast of Edinburgh and although enjoying the excitement he caused, Burns was not fooled by the adoration. He did hope that he might live by the power of his pen and abandon the rigours of farming, but any contacts he made proved to be unfruitful and most felt that the 'ploughman poet' should fulfil his role in life and return to the soil. By the end of the second winter in the capital, his fate was sealed. He brought the affair with Clarinda to a close, accepted the farm at Ellisland and legalised his marriage to Jean Armour.

Farmer once more, as he moved to Dumfriesshire, Burns must have felt wistful about what might have been. What were his feelings as he 'backward cast his e'e'?

Last days in Dumfriesshire

When Burns settled at Ellisland in 1788 with Jean Armour and the beginnings of their family, little did he know he had only eight years of life left. Into those few years he seems to have packed a lifetime. Farmer, exciseman, husband, father and collector of Scottish song, he still found time for friends and the geniality of the Dumfriesshire inns. It has been said that in this latter half of his life, his talent was whittled away writing, altering and collecting Scottish songs, but that ignores his huge contribution to Scotland's cultural history. It also ignores some of his finest works such as 'Tam o' Shanter', 'Ae Fond Kiss', 'Scots Wha Hae', 'Coming Through the Rye', 'A Man's a Man for a' That', 'The Deil's awa wi' th' Exciseman' and the beautiful 'John Anderson, My Jo'.

John Anderson, My Jo

John Anderson, my jo, John,	*love, darling*
When we were first acquent,	
Your locks were like the raven,	
Your bonie brow was brent;	*unwrinkled*
But now your brow is beld, John,	*bald*
Your locks are like the snaw;	
But blessings on your frosty pow,	*white head*

John Anderson, my jo.

John Anderson, my jo, John,	
We clamb the hill thegither;	*climbed*
And mony a canty day, John,	*happy*
We've had wi' ane anither;	
Now we maun totter down, John:	
And hand in hand we'll go,	
And sleep thegither at the foot,	
John Anderson, my Jo.	

While he was not the same man who had produced the great poems of the Mossgiel days, Burns was still master of his art. His pen was no less sharp, no less deep, if a little sadder and perhaps wiser.

> Life is but a Day at most;
> Sprung from Night – in Darkness lost:
> Hope not Sunshine every hour,
> Fear not Clouds will ever lour.
> Happiness is but a name,
> Make Content and Ease thy aim.
> Ambition is a meteor-gleam;
> Fame, a restless idle dream;
> **(Written in Friars' Carse Hermitage: first version)**

He never lost his vigour for life, or his insight, nor was his love of nature or his fellow man any less acute. And his tributes to the 'lasses' continued. At this point you could quote from 'Ae Fond Kiss' or 'O Whistle and I'll come to you, my Lad'. Remember 'Ae Fond Kiss' was written in 1791 as a final farewell to 'Clarinda', and the yearning in it signifies not only the pain of a lost love but is also an elegy to his lost hope.

Ae Fond Kiss

Ae fond kiss, and then we sever;   *One*
Ae fareweel, and then for ever!
Deep in heart-wrung tears I'll pledge thee,
Warring sighs and groans I'll wage thee.

Who shall say that Fortune grieves him
While the star of hope she leaves him?
Me, nae cheerful twinkle lights me:
Dark despair around benights me.

I'll ne'er blame my partial fancy,
Naething could resist my Nancy:
But to see her was to love her;
Love but her, and love for ever.

Had we never lov'd sae kindly!
Had we never lov'd sae blindly!
Never met – or never parted,
We had ne'er been broken-hearted.

Fare-thee-weel, thou first and fairest!
Fare-thee-weel, thou best and dearest!
Thine be ilka joy and treasure,   *every*
Peace, Enjoyment, Love and Pleasure!

Ae fond kiss, and then we sever!

> Ae fareweel, Alas, for ever!
> Deep in heart-wrung tears I'll pledge thee,
> Warring sighs and groans I'll wage thee.

At the end Burns must have looked back on his Dumfriesshire days with some fondness and contentment. Although his dreams of making a living by his art were long gone and the physical demands of his work had taken their toll on his health, Burns knew there were compensations in his wife and children and the support of true friends. Although often struck down by melancholic moods, he could always find humour in life's little ironies and incongruities. In the midst of problems and pain they lifted his spirits and allowed him to laugh at the ridiculousness of life. That is the common ground between Burns and those who share his beliefs.

Summing up – *Burns's contribution*

When we consider his chronic health problems and his difficult, often treacherous working conditions, we can only wonder at Burns's contribution to Scottish literature and life. We cannot emulate his greatness, but we can take heart from his courage, find compassion for our fellow man and hope for the future. Burns's work advocates living life to the full, being kind to one's neighbour, enjoying the simple pleasures and feeling grateful for the privilege. His maxim from 'Epistle to Davie' best describes the man and his philosophy:

> The heart ay's the part ay   *always*
> That makes us right or wrang.

The speech should finish with the toast:

> 'Ladies and Gentlemen I give you "The Immortal Memory of Robert Burns".'

BURNS'S WIT

Introduction — *Burns's wit: forte or foible?*

Burns's wit flowed through all his writing and conversation. It was at times corrective, at others gentle and teasing and when directed at himself, as poet and rhymer, it was pure tongue-in-cheek humour. Burns's wit stemmed from his instinctive love of life and all its idiosyncracies. Pretension, hypocrisy and greed often caused his hackles to rise and many felt the force of his passion and anger.

From his early days of debate at the Tarbolton Bachelors' Club, through the heady days in Edinburgh society, to the final sallies at Dumfries, Burns never lost his passion for the lightning thrust in conversation or the stinging barb in verse. That would have been to deny his instincts. Maria Riddell, who suffered more than most from the blows of his sharp pen, revealed in her splendid obituary to Burns that she believed that poetry was not actually his forte, but that the cut and thrust of social encounter was where he reigned supreme:

> Many others, perhaps, may have ascended to prouder heights
> in the region of Parnassus, but none certainly ever outshone
> Burns in the charms, the sorcery, I would almost call it, of
> fascinating conversation, the spontaneous eloquence of social
> argument, or the unstudied poignancy of brilliant repartee.
>
> The rapid lightnings of his eye were always the harbingers of
> some flash of genius, whether they darted the fiery glances of
> insulted and indignant superiority, or beamed with the
> impassioned sentiment of fervent and impetuous affections.

The keenness of his satire was, I am almost at a loss whether to say, his forte or his foible, for though nature had endowed him with a portion of the most pointed excellence in that dangerous talent, he suffered it too often to be the vehicle of personal, and sometimes unfounded, animosities.

He paid for his mischievious wit as dearly as anyone could do. 'Twas no extravagant arithmetic', to say of him, as was said of Yorick, 'that for every ten jokes he got a hundred enemies'.

(From Maria Riddell's obituary, *Dumfries Advertiser, 31 July 1796*)

This testimony to his talents could be summed up in one line from his poem 'Epistle from Esopus to Maria' – 'A wit in folly and a fool in wit'.

Certainly Burns's reputation for delivering the sharp rebuke went before him and there were always those ill at ease in his company. But equally his charm was just as devastating and he often left the same company bedazzled by it.

So, was satire Burns's forte or foible? You could begin by looking at Burns's extremes of wit in verse with two examples from his Dumfriesshire days. The first is a spiteful verse he coined about Maria Riddell's carriage (see also 'Monody on a lady famed for her caprice') after the row which broke up their friendship for a time:

> If you rattle along like your mistress's tongue,
> Your speed will out-rival the dart;
> But, a fly for your load, you'll break down on the road,
> If your stuff be as rotten's her heart.

> *(Extempore, pinned to a lady's coach)*

and the second, a light, amusing epitaph he suggested for a friend's tombstone:

> Beneath this turn lies W . . . G . . .
> Nature thy loss bemoan;
> When thou wouldst make a fool again
> Thy choicest model's gone.
>
> (From Gordon Irving, *The Wit of Robert Burns*)

Burns's sojourn in Edinburgh produced many exclamations about his eloquence, wit and vigour in conversation and his pen was no less active either, whether in taking some presumptuous host or hostess down a peg or two or simply praising a fair lady. His description of Miss Burnet, Lord Monboddo's daughter, for example, in a letter to a friend, was typical of the extreme flights to which he was prone when confronted with great beauty:

> There has not been anything nearly like her in all the
> combinations of Beauty, Grace and Goodness, the great Creator
> has formed since Milton's Eve on the first day of her existence.
>
> *(Letter to William Chambers, Edinburgh, 27 December 1786)*

But the same pen wrote, in very different terms, to an eminent peeress in Edinburgh who, though never having met the poet, was desperate to have him exhibited at one of her soirées. Remembering that at the time an animal called 'The Learned Pig' was being displayed for the crowd's amusement in the Grassmarket, he replied wickedly to her invitation:

> Mr Burns will do himself the honour of waiting on Her
> Ladyship provided she will invite also 'The Learned Pig'.
>
> (From Gordon Irving, *The Wit of Robert Burns*)

Maria Riddell's question of his wit being forte or foible could be applied to any area of Burns's writing. The following on the Church, women and himself are only suggestions.

Development – *The Church*

The poet's dislike of hypocrisy and the unrealistic strictures of the religion of the day often brought him into conflict with the Church, the clergy and pillars of the community. Verses from any of his three great satires against the Church, 'Holy Willie's Prayer', 'Address to the Unco Guid', or 'The Holy Fair', could be used. In the following verses Burns delivers a salutary slap on the wrist to the parishioners of Mauchline for their conceit and unchristian attitudes:

> Ye high, exalted, virtuous Dames,
> Ty'd up in godly laces,
> Before ye gie poor *Frailty* names,
> Suppose a change o' cases;
> A dear-lov'd lad, convenience snug,
> A treacherous inclination –
> But, let me whisper i' your lug,   *ear*
> Ye're aiblins nae temptation.   *perhaps*
>
> Then gently scan your brother Man,
> Still gentler sister Woman;
> Tho' they may gang a kennin wrang,
> To step aside is human:
> One point must still be greatly dark,
> The moving *Why* they do it;
> And just as lamely can ye mark,
> How far perhaps they rue it.
>
> (*Address to the Unco Guid, or the Rigidly Righteous*)

You could also include this lighter nudge at the clergy, as Burns devilishly suggests what lies behind their sanctimonious façade:

> The minister kiss't the fiddler's wife
> He could na preach for thinkin o't.
>
> *(My Love she's but a Lassie Yet)*

What should be emphasized, if speaking on this aspect of his work, is that Burns, underneath all his denunciations of the Church, was a devout believer in God and the concept of Christianity. What he railed against, apart from the false piety it engendered (beautifully illustrated in 'Holy Willie's Prayer'), was the manipulation, by fear, of an ignorant and superstitious populate. Too practical and intelligent to be indoctrinated into passivity, he often appeared to many as an atheist and a reactionary.

The lasses

If looking at the 'lasses', consult the speaker delivering 'The Toast to the Lasses' in case your material overlaps.

Burns's love of the 'lasses' is well documented, both in his life and work. They were the inspiration for his best romantic verse and they played a vital part in his existence. The following are just a few of his comments to and about women. Finding himself sitting next to pretty Miss Ainslie in church and listening to the minister loudly condemn 'obstinate sinners', Burns quickly dashed off this compliment and handed it to her:

> Fair maid, you need not take the hint,
> Nor idle texts pursue;
> 'Twas guilty sinners that he meant –
> Not angels such as you.
>
> *(To Miss Ainslie, while looking for a text in church)*

Their tricks an' craft hae put me daft,
They've ta'en me in, an' a' that;
But clear your decks, an' here's the Sex!
I like the jads for a' that.   *jades*
    (*The Jolly Beggars*)

There's ae wee faut they whiles lay to me,
I like the lasses – Gude forgie me!
For mony a plack they wheedle frae me   *coin*
At dance or fair;
Maybe some other thing they gie me,
They weel can spare.
    (*Epistle to J. Lapraik*)

His wit about women is very different from that about the Church. There is nothing he would change about the 'lasses'. He, unlike many men, then and now, doesn't feel threatened by them. They and all their intricacies are a constant source of delight. To finish this theme and lead into the next you could recite 'Advice to the Mauchline Belles'. In this poem Burns casts himself in the role of the fox in the farmyard.

O leave novels, ye Mauchline belles,
Ye're safer at your spinning-wheel;
Such witching books are baited hooks
For rakish rooks like Rob Mossgiel;
Your fine Tom Jones and Grandisons,
They make your youthful fancies reel;
They heat your brains, and fire your veins,
And then you're prey for Rob Mossgiel.

Beware a tongue that's smoothly hung,
A heart that warmly seems to feel;

That feeling heart but acts a part –
'Tis rakish art in Rob Mossgiel.
The frank address, the soft caress,
Are worse than poisoned darts of steel;
The frank address, and politesse,
Are all finesse in Rob Mossgiel.

Burns on himself

Burns's wit about himself takes many forms. There are the marvellously relaxed, seemingly casually construed lines in 'Extempore Epistle to Gavin Hamilton, Esq.' (stanzas on 'naething'):

The Poet may jingle and rhyme
In hopes of a laureate wreathing,
And when he has wasted his time
He's kindly rewarded with naething.

And now, I must mount on the wave,
My voyage perhaps there is death in:
What is a watery grave?
The drowning a Poet is naething.

In another poem, 'Epistle to J. Lapraik', a smiling assurance is evident:

I am nae poet, in a sense,
But just a rhymer like by chance;
An' hae to learning nae pretence;
Yet, what the matter?
Whene'er my muse does on me glance,
I jingle at her.

> Your critic-folk may cock their nose,
> And say, 'How can you e'er propose,
> You wha ken hardly verse frae prose,
> To mak a sang?'
> But, by your leaves, my learned foes,
> Ye're maybe wrang.
>
> Gie me ae spark o' nature's fire,
> That's a' the learning I desire;
> Then tho' I drudge thro' dub an' mire   *puddles*
> At pleugh or cart,
> My muse, tho' hamely in attire,
> May touch the heart.

In all these verses Burns's light touch shows his complete mastery of wry humour. His mockery of the poet's life and all its contrariness also reveals that had he the choice, he would change 'naething'. The last verse from 'Epistle to a Young Friend' is magnanimous Burns at his best:

> Adieu, dear, amiable Youth!
> Your heart can ne'er be wanting!
> May Prudence, Fortitude, and Truth,
> Erect your brow undaunting!
> In ploughman phrase, 'God send you speed'
> Still daily to grow wiser;
> And may ye better reck the rede,   *attend to the advice*
> Than ever did th' Adviser.

Summing up – *Wit and wisdom*

In summing up Burns's wit, whether you decide it was forte or foible, you could suggest that the core of it comes from his roots in the soil of Ayrshire.

As a farmer, Burns's constant companions were death, disease and destruction or alternatively the abundance of a plentiful harvest, the beauty of a summer day or the sensuous charms of a pretty woman. These extremities polarised his thought. He had little time for the affectation or unkindness born out of idle minds. He loved beauty, both the physical and the spiritual, and in hypocrisy, greed and conceit he found only ugliness. He used his wit as a whiplash against anything and anyone he found wanting in the warmth of human compassion, but equally he applauded life's fleeting joys, held up to the light its extremities of behaviour and hoped that someday:

> That Man to Man, the world o'er,
> Shall brothers be for a' that!
> *(A Man's a Man for a' That)*

You should finish the speech with thoughts of what we can learn today from Burns's work and wisdom, remembering that wit was only one arrow in his quiver.

The speech should finish with the toast: 'Ladies and Gentlemen I give you "The Immortal Memory of Robert Burns"

PLOUGHMAN POET OR INTELLECTUAL?

Edinburgh dubbed Burns the 'ploughman poet' during his first visit to the city, after the publication of the Kilmarnock edition of his work in 1786. Initially mistaken for some inspired rustic, a notion he enjoyed perpetrating, it quickly became obvious that, although an Ayrshire farmer, he was wisely schooled and widely read, possessed of a fine mind, an observant eye and a lively tongue. At any gathering his companions could find themselves either damned or charmed, depending on his level of sufferance.

Introduction – *The different sides of Burns's talent*

You could begin this theme with Lord Byron's description of Burns's diversities of mind, after reading the unpublished letters:

> They are full of oaths and obscene songs. What an antithetical mind! – tenderness, toughness – delicacy, coarseness sentiment, sensuality – soaring and grovelling, dirt and deity – all mixed up in that one compound of inspired clay!

In many ways that 'compound of inspired clay' typifies the Scottish character and its extremes of existence, the combination of practicality and emotion. One reason for Burns's immediate success was that the majority of the population recognised in themselves and their lives, all that Burns had dared to record on paper.

But Burns's literary insights did not just tumble from his pen. They were the result of a great deal of thought and effort. His early masterpieces were composed in the fields during the day and in the evening harnessed, refined and honed to perfection. 'Ploughman poet' perhaps, but his work was also a potent combination of innate surety, a solid education, a childhood imagination stimulated by old Scots songs and tales, and hours of polishing and reassessing his thoughts. Behind the seeming naivety and deceptive simplicity of his best-known work lies the hand of a master craftsman.

To illustrate this contrast you could quote verses from 'The Rigs o' Barley' and 'Death and Dr Hornbook', both from the Ayrshire years. Each show a different side of his talent:

It was upon a Lammas night,
When corn rigs are bonie,
Beneath the moon's unclouded light,
I held awa to Annie;
The time flew by, wi' tentless heed,
Till 'tween the late and early,
Wi' sma' persuasion she agreed
To see me thro' the barley.

The sky was blue, the wind was still,
The moon was shining clearly;
I set her down, wi' right good will,
Amang the rigs o' barley:
I ken't her heart was a' my ain;
I lov'd her most sincerely;
I kiss'd her owre and owre again,
Amang the rigs o' barley.

(The Rigs o' Barley)

Burns describes the heady pleasures of a warm summer's evening, but equally, with consummate skill, in 'Death and Dr Hornbook', he sets the scene, albeit tongueincheek, for a supernatural tale:

But this that I am gaun to tell,   *going*
Which lately on a night befel,
Is just as true's the Deil's in hell
Or Dublin city:
That e'er he nearer comes oursel
'S a muckle pity.

The clachan yill had made me canty,   *village ale   merry*

I was na fou, but just had plenty;   *drunk*
I stacher'd whyles, but yet took tent ay   *staggered at times*
                                                                    care
To free the ditches;
An' hillocks, stanes, an' bushes, kenn'd ay
Frae ghaists an' witches.

The rising moon began to glowre   *stare*
The distant Cumnock hill out-owre:
To count her horns, wi' a' my pow'r,
I set myself;
But whether she had three or four,
I cou'd na tell.

Development – *Ploughman poet or intellectual*

You could say that Burns was 'ploughman poet' in that he found his
inspiration in the countryside and the people he came into contact with in
the daily round of rural life. But, just as importantly, this was the
background in which his character was formed: the disciplines he endured,
both behind the plough and as he worked late into the night with his pen,
saw Burns through his most difficult days.

It was that character, combined with a commanding presence and great
personal charm, which earned him as many laurels in Edinburgh as his
poetry had done.

In great demand, he enjoyed airing his sharp wit and intellect, impressing
the university's professors, overpowering the city burghers and being the
'darling' of society. By the time Burns left Edinburgh for Dumfriesshire,
the powers of his intellect could hardly be in doubt. But 'ploughman poet'

he was and so he would stay. We look back now and wonder why, after so much critical acclaim and adulation, nothing was done to help Burns live by his writing, why indeed Scotland so rarely rewards its own. Perhaps his wit was just too sharp.

Edinburgh, fortunately, had little effect on his work: for he refused advice, often given, to write in English and continued instead to communicate in the language of the people. His later works in Dumfriesshire show that he had not lost his touch in his ability to appeal directly to the heart or mind. You could recite verses from the stirring 'Scots Wha Hae' ('Bruce to his men at Bannockburn'):

> Scots, wha hae wi' Wallace bled,   *who have*
> Scots, wham Bruce has aften led,   *whom*
> Welcome to your gory bed,
> Or to victorie!
>
> By oppressions's woes and pains!
> By your sons in servile chains!
> We will drain our dearest veins,
> But they shall be free!
>
> Lay the proud usurpers low!
> Tyrants fall in ev'ry foe!
> Liberty's in ev'ry blow! –
> Let us do or die!

Or the rousing 'The Deil's awa wi' th' Exciseman':

> The Deil's awa, the deil's awa,
> The Deil's awa wi' th' Exciseman,

He's danc'd awa, he's danc'd awa,
He's danc'd awa wi' th' Exciseman.

We'll mak our maut and we'll brew our drink,
We'll laugh, sing and rejoice, man!
And mony braw thanks to the meikle black Deil *hearty – big*
That danc'd awa wi' th' Exciseman.

There's threesome reels, there's foursome reels,
There's hornpipes and strathspeys, man,
But the ae best dance e'er cam to the Land,
Was 'The Deil's awa wi' th' Exciseman'.

Summing up – *Burns: a unique poet*

By the end of this speech it should be apparent that the 'ploughman poet' cannot be separated from the intellectual. You should point out that Burns has a unique place in Scotland's literary history, in keeping alive the traditional Scots language used by his predecessors Allan Ramsay and Robert Fergusson. Burns's education in rural Ayrshire, made possible by his father's fervent belief in learning (and he was not alone in this), ensured that he was not only on a par with those he met in the capital but in most cases superior.

Burns was a ploughman poet, to all intents and purposes, not in the patronising terms of the Edinburgh burghers, but in the sense that his work affected his whole being and strengthened his passions and beliefs. But he was also an intellectual in his ability to translate life's pain and passion into something beautiful and enduring and to try to make some order, however strained, out of man's existence. That is why we gather to celebrate his life. 'Ploughman poet' or intellectual, it does not really matter. It is the man and his courage in a hard-fought fight that we salute.

The speech should finish with the toast: 'Ladies and Gentlemen I give you "The Immortal Memory of Robert Burns".'

THE OTHER SPEECHES

APPRECIATION OF 'THE IMMORTAL MEMORY'

After 'The Immortal Memory' is delivered, the piper plays a tune, and then a short 'Appreciation' of the speech is usually given, either by a guest or the Chairman himself. It has the dual role of being a thank you to the speaker for his skill and insight and a further opportunity to reflect on Burns's life and work and how it can inspire us today. 'The Appreciation' should last no longer than five minutes and should really be given by someone with a wide knowledge of Burns.

'The Appreciation' is followed by the two other compulsory speeches, 'The Toast to the Lasses' and 'The Reply'. These should last no longer than ten minutes and should change the mood of the evening from serious thought to amusement and hilarity.

'THE TOAST TO THE LASSES'

As explained earlier, this toast was originally a thank you to the ladies for preparing the food for the evening and a time to toast the 'lasses' in Burns's life. Today's audience will expect to hear a witty speech about the female sex, with a few nudges and sly digs about their idiosyncrasies and foibles. It shouldn't be offensive and should end on a conciliatory note. The speech should blend modern observations with quotations and sentiments from Burns's work. You could use examples from the poet's work, showing that the 'lasses' were just as difficult to understand in his day. Kate, Tam o' Shanter's wife, deserves a mention as perhaps does Willie Wastle's wife. Clarinda and Maria Riddell drove Burns to heights of frenzy and frustration. In 'Monody (on a lady famed for her caprice)' the full force of Burns's satire is unleashed on Maria Riddell, but in 'The Last Time I Came o'er the Moor' he describes his despair and exasperation with this woman, and how she has affected him. Emotions not unknown in both sexes.

The Last Time I Came O'er the Moor

The last time I came o'er the moor,
And left Maria's dwelling,
What throes, what tortures passing cure,
Were in my bosom swelling:
Condemned to see my rival's reign,
While I in secret languish;
To feel a fire in every vein,
Yet dare not speak my anguish.

Love's veriest wretch, despairing, I
Fain, fain my crime would cover:
The unweeting groan, the bursting sigh,   *unwitting*
Betray the guilty lover.
I know my doom must be despair:
Thou wilt nor canst relieve me;
But, O Maria, hear my prayer,
For pity's sake, forgive me!

The music of thy tongue I heard,
Nor wist while it enslaved me;
I saw thine eyes, yet nothing feared,
Till fears no more had saved me.
The unwary sailor thus, aghast,
The wheeling torrent viewing,
Mid circling horrors yields at last
In overwhelming ruin!

Frustrated, thwarted, or simply baffled, Burns adored the 'lasses' and you should finish this speech with a tribute to them before asking the men to rise and drink: 'The Toast to the Lasses'.

THE REPLY

'The Reply' from the 'lasses' should also be a humorous speech, in turn detailing men's vices and lack of virtue. You could quote from 'Tam o' Shanter':

And at his elbow, Souter Johnny,   *Cobbler*
His ancient, trusty, drouthy, crony;   *thirsty*
Tam lo'ed him like a very brither;
They had been fou for weeks thegither.   *drunk*
The night drave on wi' sangs and clatter;
And ay the ale was growing better:
The Landlady and Tam grew gracious
Wi' favours secret, sweet and precious:

You could also quote from 'Willie brew'd a Peck o' Maut' where Burns beautifully describes the idiocy produced by alcohol, as the three cronies insist they are not drunk:

We are na fou, we're nae that fou,   *drunk*
But just a drappie in our e'e;   *drop – eye*
The cock may craw, the day may daw, *dawn*
And ay we'll taste the barley bree.   *brew, juice*

Here are we met, three merry boys,
Three merry boys, I trow, are we;
And mony a night we've merry been,
And mony mae we hope to be!   *more*

Again, like the previous speech, after pointing out the imperfections of the opposite sex, it should end on a conciliatory note, but leaving no doubt as to where Burns's allegiance lay.

When ance life's day draws near the gloamin, *once*
Then fareweel vacant, careless roamin; *twilight*
An' fareweel cheerfu' tankards foamin,
An' social noise:
An' fareweel dear, deluding woman,
The joy of joys!

(Epistle to James Smith)

OTHER TOASTS

At many suppers there is a toast to the town or city and a toast to 'Scotland' or 'Scotia' is popular. At dinners abroad it is common to toast Scotland, but also the adopted country. Other frequent toasts within the Burns Club Federation are the Federation itself or 'Kindred clubs'. If you have a Federation representative at your supper, invite him or her to reply and ask them to explain about the organisation and its aims.

POEMS AND SONGS

Once the speeches are over the evening continues with songs and recitations from Burns's work. They should contrast with one another to create different moods from the gentle intimacy of 'To a Mouse' to the rollicking fun of 'The Deil's awa wi' th' Exciseman'. Standard favourites for recitations are 'Tam o' Shanter', 'Holy Willie's Prayer', 'Address to the Unco Guid, or the Rigidly Righteous' and 'To a Mouse', but others such as 'The Auld Farmer's New Year Morning Salutation to his Auld Mare, Maggie', 'Death and Dr Hornbook', 'Extempore Epistle to Gavin Hamilton' and 'The Twa Dogs' are equally enjoyed.

Any of Burns's songs can be sung. The singers will have suggestions and know which they perform best. 'A Red, Red Rose', 'The Banks o' Doon', 'Willie brew'd a Peck o' Maut', 'Ca' the Yowes to the Knowes', 'O Whistle, and I'll come to you, my Lad' and 'A Highland Lad my love was Born' from 'The Jolly Beggars' are all popular choices. Each singer sings two or three songs and there is usually one duet.

In the following pages you will find some of these poems and songs with notes on their origins. Whichever you choose for your evening's entertainment, you could, after introducing the speaker or singer, give a brief history of each poem and song before it is performed.

Alloway Kirkyard

TAM O' SHANTER

A favourite at every dinner, Burns's tall tale is a splendid piece of entertainment and a fine example of his fertile imagination. The story that Burns wrote it in one day (late in 1790) as he walked up and down the banks of the River Nith behind Ellisland, must be taken with a pinch of salt. Perhaps he put the final draft together there, a feverish mental activity seems captured in the pace of the poem. It's been said that Jean Armour always maintained that Burns spent the day by the river and that she could hear him laughing and howling with delight. Listening to it delivered by a good speaker you will find yourself carried along by the speed of the action and consequently exhausted at the finish. Rousing, amusing and with the gently wagging finger at the end, it is a complete work of art in every sense.

No doubt Burns found inspiration in many places for the action, the characters and the setting, but we know that it came about at the instigation of Francis Grose when he was looking for a supernatural tale for inclusion in the second volume of his *Antiquities of Scotland*, published in 1791. In exchange for Grose's promise to include a drawing of Alloway Kirkyard, where his father was buried, Burns produced his ripping yarn to accompany the illustration.

The source of his inspiration came from earlier days in Ayrshire. Alloway's supposedly haunted kirkyard provided an eerie backdrop for Tam's meeting with the other world and the characters of Tam and his crony Souter Johnny were based on two individuals whom Burns remembered from his Kirkoswald days.

Shanter was the name of a farm steading between Turnberry and Culzean and the farmer Douglas Graham was the model for Tam. Given to drinking late in the pubs in Ayr after the markets closed, Graham and his friend John Davidson (Souter Johnny) often rolled home the worse for wear. Graham's wife complained about these constant binges, warning they would end in disaster one day.

Thus Graham provided Burns with the theme of the poem and the setting of Alloway's haunted kirkyard. After one of his market-day trips he lost his bonnet with the day's takings inside. Trembling at the thought of explaining to his wife, he made up a tale (plausible he believed, in his drunken stupor) about being set upon by witches in the churchyard. 'Cutty Sark' was also based on a Kirkoswald woman, Kate Stein, a fortune teller reputed to be a witch.

Tam o' Shanter
A Tale

'Of Brownyis and of Bogillis full is this Buke.'
Gawin Douglas

When chapman billies leave the street   *packman fellows*

And drouthy neebors neebors meet;   *thirsty*
As market days are wearing late,
An' folk begin to tak the gate;   *road*
While we sit bousing at the nappy,   *ale*
An' gettin fou and unco happy,   *drunk – very*
We think na on the lang Scots miles,
The mosses, waters, slaps, and stiles,   *bogs – gaps*
That lie between us and our hame,
Whare sits our sulky sullen dame,
Gathering her brows like gathering storm,
Nursing her wrath to keep it warm.

This truth fand honest Tam o' Shanter,   *found*
As he frae Ayr ae night did canter:
(Auld Ayr, wham ne'er a town surpasses
For honest men and bonny lasses).

O Tam! hadst thou but been sae wise
As taen thy ain wife Kate's advice!
She tauld thee weel thou was a skellum,   *rogue*
A blethering, blustering drunken blellum;
That frae November till October
Ae market-day thou was na sober;

That ilka melder wi' the miller   *every*
Thou sat as lang as thou had siller;   *money*
That every naig was ca'd a shoe on   *shod*
The smith and thee gat roaring fou on;
That at the L—d's house, ev'n on Sunday,
Thou drank wi' Kirkton Jean till Monday.
She prophesy'd that, late or soon,

Thou wad be found deep drown'd in Doon;
Or catch'd wi' warlocks in the mirk   *wizards –*
                                                  darkness
By Alloway's auld haunted kirk.

Ah, gentle dames! it gars me greet   *makes – weeps*
To think how mony counsels sweet,
How mony lengthen'd, sage advices
The husband from the wife despises!

But to our tale: – Ae market night,
Tam had got planted unco right;
Fast by an ingle, bleezing finely,   *fire*
Wi' reaming swats, that drank divinely;   *foaming – new ale*
And at his elbow, Souter Johnny,   *Cobbler*
His ancient, trusty, drouthy crony,   *thirsty*
Tam lo'ed him like a very brither;
They had been fou for weeks thegither.
The night drave on wi' sangs and clatter;
And ay the ale was growing better:
The Landlady and Tam grew gracious
Wi' favours secret, sweet and precious:
The Souter tauld his queerest stories;
The landlord's laugh was ready chorus:
The storm without might rair and rustle,   *roar*
Tam did na mind the storm a whistle.

Care, mad to see a man sae happy,
E'en drown'd himself amang the nappy;
As bees flee hame wi' lades o' treasure,   *loads*
The minutes wing'd their way wi' pleasure:

Kings may be blest, but Tam was glorious,
O'er a' the ills o' life victorious!
But pleasures are like poppies spread,
You seize the flowr, its bloom is shed;
Or like the snow falls in the river,
A moment white – then melts for ever;
Or like the borealis race
That flit ere you can point their place,
Or like the rainbows lovely form
Evanishing amid the storm.
Nae man can tether time or tide;
The hour approaches Tam maun ride;   *must*
That hour o' night's black arch the key-stane,
That dreary hour he mounts his beast in;
And sic a night he taks the road in
As ne'er poor sinner was abroad in.

The wind blew as 'twad brawn its last;   *would have*
The rattling show'rs rose on the blast;
The speedy gleams the darkness swallow'd;
Loud, deep, and lang, the thunder bellow'd:
That night a child might understand
The Deil had business on his hand.

Weel mounted on his gray mare, Meg,
A better never lifted leg,
Tam skelpit on thro' dub and mire,   *rattled – puddle*
Despising wind, and rain, and fire;
Whiles holding fast his gude blue bonnet;
Whiles crooning o'er some auld Scots sonnet;   *humming*
Whiles glow'ring round wi' prudent cares   *gazing*

Lest bogles catch him unawares: *hobgoblins*
Kirk-Alloway was drawing nigh,
Whare ghaists and houlets nightly cry.   *owls*

By this time he was' cross the ford,
Whare in the snaw the chapman smoor'd;   *smothered*
And past the birks and meikle stane   *birches – big*
Whare drunken Charlie brak's neck-bane;
And thro' the whins, and by the cairn   *gorse – pile of stones*
Whare hunters fand the murder'd bairn;   *child*
And near the thorn, aboon the well,   *above*
Whare Mungo's mither hang'd hersel.
Before him Doon pours all his floods,
The doubling storm roars thro' the woods;
The lightnings flash frae pole to pole;
Near and more near the thunders roll:
When, glimmering thro' the groaning trees,
Kirk-Alloway seem'd in a bleeze;
Thro' ilka bore the beams were glancing;   *every cranny*
And loud resounded mirth and dancing.

Inspiring bold John Barleycorn!
What dangers thou canst make us scorn!
Wi' tippenny we fear nae evil;
Wi' usquabae we'll face the devil!   *whisky*
The swats sae ream'd in Tammie's noddle,
Fair play, he car'd na deils a boddle.
But Maggie stood right sair astonish'd,
Till, by the heel and hand admonish'd,
She ventur'd forward on the light;

And, vow! Tam saw an unco sight   *in sooth! – marvellous*
Warlocks and witches in a dance;
Nae cotillion brent new frae France,   *brand-new*
But hornpipes, jigs, strathspeys and reels,
Put life and mettle in their heels.
A winnock-bunker in the east,   *window-recess*
There sat auld Nick, in shape o' beast;
A towzie tyke, black, grim and large,   *shaggy dog*
To gie them music was his charge:
He screw'd the pipes and gart them skirl   *made – scream*
Till roof and rafters a' did dirl.   *vibrate*
Coffins stood round, like open presses,   *cupboards*
That shaw'd the dead in their last dresses;
And, by some devilish cantraip sleight,   *weird trick*
Each in its cauld hand held a light –
By which heroic Tam was able
To note upon the haly table
A murderer's banes, in gibbet-airns;   *irons*
Twa span-lang, wee, unchristen'd bairns;
A thief new-cutted frae a rape,   *from a rope*
Wi' his last gasp his gab did gape;   *mouth*
Five tomahawks wi' blude red-rusted;
Five scymitars wi' murder crusted;
A garter which a babe had strangled;
A knife a father's throat had mangled –
Whom his ain son o' life bereft –
The grey hairs yet stack to the heft;   *stuck to the handle*
Wi' mair of horrible and awefu',
Which ev'n to name wad be unlawfu'.

As Tammie glowr'd, amaz'd and curious,   *stared*

The mirth and fun grew fast and furious:
The piper loud and louder blew,
The dancers quick and quicker flew:
They reel'd, they set, they cross'd, they cleekit, *took hands*
Till ilka carlin swat and reekit, *witch — steamed*
And coost her duddies to the wark, *threw off — clothes*
And linket at it in her sark! *set to it — shift*

Now Tam, O Tam! had thae been queans, *these —*
A' plump and strapping in their teens! *young women*
Their sarks, instead o' creeshie flannen, *greasy flannel*
Been snaw white seventeen hunder linnen! —
Thir breeks o' mine, my only pair, *These —*
That ance were plush, o' gude blue hair,
I wad hae gi'en them off my hurdies *buttocks*
For ae blink o' the bonie burdies! *birds*

But wither'd beldams, auld and droll,
Rigwoodie hags wad spean a foal,
Lowping and flinging on a crummock, *leaping — stick with a*
I wonder didna turn thy stomach. *crooked head*
But Tam kend what was what fu' brawlie: *quite well*
There was ae winsome wench and wawlie, *comely*
That night enlisted in the core *corps*
(Lang after kend on Carrick shore:
For mony a beast to dead she shot, *death*
And perish'd mony a bonny boat,
And shook baith meikle corn and bear, *much barley*
And held the country-side in fear).
Her cutty sark, o' Paisley harn, *short shift — coarse linen*
That while a lassie she had worn,

In longitude tho' sorely scanty,
It was her best, and she was vauntie.   *proud of it*
Ah! little kend thy reverend grannie,
That sark she coft for her wee Nannie,   *bought*
Wi' two pund Scots ('twas a' her riches),   *3s. 6d. English*
Wad ever grac'd a dance of witches!

But here my Muse her wing maun cour   *fold*
Sic flights are far beyond her pow'r;
To sing how Nannie lap and flang   *leaped – kicked*
(A souple jade she was and strang),
And how Tam stood like ane bewitch'd
And thought his very een enrich'd;
Even Satan glowr'd, and fidg'd fu' fain,
And hotch'd and blew wi' might and main,   *squirmed*
Till first ae caper, syne anither,   *then*
Tam tint his reason a' thegither   *lost – altogether*
And roars out 'Weel done, Cutty-sark!'
And in an instant all was dark;
And scarcely had he Maggie rallied,
When out the hellish legion sallied.
As bees bizz out wi' angry fyke,   *fret*
When plundering herds assail their byke;   *herd-boys – nest*
As open pussie's mortal foes,   *the hare's*
When, pop! she starts before their nose;
As eager runs the market-crowd,
When 'Catch the thief!' resounds aloud;
So Maggie runs – the witches follow,
Wi' mony an eldritch skreech and hollow.   *frightful*
Ah, Tam! Ah, Tam! thou'll get thy fairin!   *reward, treat*

In hell they'll roast thee like a herrin!
In vain thy Kate awaits thy comin!
Kate soon will be a woefu' woman!
Now, do thy speedy utmost, Meg,
And win the key-stane of the brig;   *reach*
There, at them thou thy tail may toss:
A running stream they dare na cross.
But ere the key-stane she could make,
The fient a tail she had to shake!   *No tail had she*
For Nannie, far before the rest,
Hard upon noble Maggie prest,
And flew at Tam wi' furious ettle: *endeavour*
But little wist she Maggie's mettle –
Ae spring brought off her master hale,   *whole*
But left behind her ain grey tail:
The carlin claught her by the rump,   *clutched*
And left poor Maggie scarce a stump.

Now, wha this tale o' truth shall read,
Ilk man and mother's son, take heed:
Whene'er to drink you are inclin'd,
Or cutty sarks run in your mind,
Think! ye may buy the joys o'er dear,
Remember Tam o' Shanter's mare.

O WHISTLE, AND I'LL COME TO YOU, MY LAD

Completed in 1793 during the Dumfriesshire years, this song was written
for Jean Lorimer, a local beauty, daughter of a successful farmer, whose land

lay across the River Nith from Ellisland. Burns later changed the last line of the chorus to 'Thy Jeanie will venture wi' you, my lad', saying Jean had insisted on it. A regular visitor to her home, Kemmishall, Burns, undoubtedly inspired by her looks and spirited personality, described her as 'a fair dame whom the Graces have attired in witchcraft, and whom the Loves have armed with lightning'. She is 'The Lassie wi' the Lint-white Locks', the heroine of 'Craigieburn Wood' and his 'Chloris' in other songs. Sadly the fates which Burns saw as bestowing so many gifts upon her in youth, deserted her in later life.

At the age of 18, the year this song was finished, she refused an offer of marriage from one of Burns's fellow excise officers, choosing instead to run away with a young Englishman named Whelpdale. After a wedding at Gretna Green they settled on a farm at Barnhill, near Moffat, but within a few months he went bankrupt and disappeared. She returned to her parents' home and seeming security, but her father's farm and his business in Dumfries failed, leaving the family penniless. Her mother became ill and died and her father suffered acute depression until his death in 1809 in Penpoint. Jean became a governess, finally reduced to working in service to support herself.

Her latter years were spent in Edinburgh as housekeeper to a family in Blacket Place. When her health began to fail and she could no longer work, her employer kindly provided her with a small flat in Nicolson Square (close to where Clarinda had lived), where she spent the rest of her days. She died in 1831 at the age of 56 and was buried in Preston Street Cemetery, Newington. Seventy years later the Edinburgh Ninety Burns Club erected a memorial granite cross over her grave with the inscription 'This stone marks the grave of Jean Lorimer, the 'Chloris' and 'Lassie wi' the Lint-white Locks' of the poet Burns. Born, 1775; died, 1831. Erected under the auspices of the Ninety Burns Club, Edinburgh, 1901'.

O Whistle, and I'll come to you, my Lad
Tune – O Whistle, and I'll come to you, my Lad

Chorus – O whistle, and I'll come to you, my lad,
　　　O whistle, and I'll come to you, my lad;
　　　Tho' father and mother and a' should gae mad,
　　　O whistle, and I'll come to you, my lad.

But warily tent, when ye come to court me,　　*watch*
And come na unless the back-yett be a-jee;　*gate – ajar*
Syne up the back-style, and let naebody see,　*Then*
And come as ye were na coming to me,
And come as ye were na coming to me.

At kirk or at market, whene'er ye meet me,
Gang by me as tho' that ye car'd nae a flie;　*Go – fly*
But steal me a blink o' your bonie black e'e,　*glance*
Yet look as ye were na looking at me,
Yet look as ye were na looking at me.

Ay vow and protest that ye carena for me,
And *whyles* ye may lightly my　*sometimes – undervalue*
　　　beauty a wee;　　　　　　*– a little*
But court na anither, tho' joking ye be,
For fear that she wyle your fancy frae me,　*lure*
For fear that she wyle your fancy frae me.

HOLY WILLIE'S PRAYER

Burns's glorious hypocrite 'Holy Willie' is still instantly recognisable
today. With wonderful irony, he delivers a lash upon his own back in every

line. One of Burns's finest pieces of work, it was written in the summer of 1785 when his landlord and friend Gavin Hamilton was finally absolved by higher church courts of not keeping the Sabbath. The chief instigator of the prosecution was William Fisher, a church elder and member of the Kirk Session of Mauchline Parish Church, which first 'tried' Hamilton for such crimes as picking potatoes on Sunday and not attending church. A Mauchline man by birth, Hamilton lived there with his wife and young family, practising as a lawyer and administering the poor fund. A kind-hearted and generous friend to many, he was the very antitheses of William Fisher.

Fisher, born the son of a farmer in 1737 became an elder of Mauchline Church in 1772. A gossiping, smug, zealous upholder of strict Calvinist tenets, he came unstuck in 1790 when he was publicly rebuked by the minister, William Auld, for drunkenness, and although there is no church record, it is also believed that he was charged with stealing from the poor box. He froze to death in a ditch near Mauchline during a blizzard on 13 February 1809.

Burns initially circulated the poem amongst friends as it was considered too strident an attack on the Church to be published. It was only in 1799, three years after his death, that it was finally printed, and then only as a leaflet, by a Glasgow publisher.

Holy Willie's Prayer
And Send the Godly in a pet to pray. – Pope

O Thou that in the heavens does dwell!
Wha, as it pleases best Thysel,
Sends ane to heaven and ten to h-ll,

A' for Thy glory;
And no for ony guid or ill
They've done before Thee!

I bless and praise Thy matchless might,
When thousands Thou hast left in night,
That I am here before Thy sight,
For gifts and grace
A burning and a shining light,
To a' this place.

What was I, or my generation,
That I should get such exaltation?
I, wha deserv'd most just damnation
For broken laws,
Sax thousand years ere my creation
Thro' Adam's cause.

When frae my mither's womb I fell,
Thou might hae plungèd me in hell,
To gnash my gums, to weep and wail,
In burnin lakes,
Where damnèd devils roar and yell,
Chain'd to their stakes.

Yet I am here, a chosen sample,
To show Thy grace is great and ample;
I'm here, a pillar o' Thy temple,
Strong as a rock;
A guide, a ruler, and example
To a' Thy flock.

O L—d, Thou kens what zeal I bear,
When drinkers drink, an' swearers swear,
An' singin' there, an' dancin' here,
Wi' great and sma';
For I am keepit by Thy fear,
Free frae them a'.

But yet, O L—d, confess I must,
At times I'm fash'd wi' fleshly lust;   *troubled*
And sometimes too in warldly trust
Vile Self gets in:
But Thou remembers we are dust,
Defiled wi' sin.

O L—d – yestreen – Thou kens – wi Meg
Thy pardon I sincerely beg:
O, may't ne'er be a livin plague,
To my dishonor!
And I'll ne'er lift a lawless leg
Again upon her!

Besides, I further maun avow,
Wi' Leezie's lass – three times – I trow
But L—d, that Friday I was fou   *drunk*
When I cam near her;
Or else, Thou kens, Thy servant true
Wad never steer her.   *meddle with*

Maybe Thou lets this fleshly thorn
Buffet Thy servant e'en and morn
Lest he owre proud and high should turn

That he's sae gifted:
If sae, Thy hand maun e'en be borne
Until Thou lift it.

L–d bless Thy chosen in this place,
For here Thou has a chosen race;
But L–d confound their stubborn face,
And blast their name,
Wha bring their rulers to disgrace
And public shame.

L–d mind Gaun Hamilton's deserts;
He drinks, and swears, and plays at cartes   *cards*
Yet has sae mony takin arts   *popular*
Wi' Great and Sma',
Frae G–d's ain Priest the people's hearts
He steals awa.

And when we chasten'd him therefore
Thou kens how he bred sic a splore,   *disturbance*
And set the warld in a roar
O' laughin at us:
Curse Thou his basket and his store
Kail and potatoes.

L–d hear my earnest cry and pray'r
Against that Presbytry of Ayr!
Thy strong right hand, L–d make it bare
Upo' their heads!
L–d visit them and dinna spare,
For their misdeeds!

O L—d, my G—d, that glib-tongu'd Aiken,
My very heart and flesh are quakin,
To think how I sat, sweatin, shakin,
And – wi' dread,
While Auld, wi' hingin lip gaed sneakin   *sneaky*
And hid his head.

L—d in Thy day o' vengeance try him!
L—d visit them wha did employ him!
And pass not in Thy mercy by them,
Nor hear their prayer,
But for Thy people's sake destroy them,
And dinna spare!

But L—d remember me and mine
Wi' mercies temporal and divine;
That I for grace and gear may shine,
Excell'd by nane!
And a' the glory shall be Thine,
AMEN! AMEN!

THE BANKS O' DOON

The story behind this song is a sad one. It is a lament for the fate of Peggy Kennedy at the hands of her 'fause lover', Captain Andrew McDowall of Logan. The daughter of Robert Kennedy of Daljarroch and a niece of the poet's friend Gavin Hamilton, Peggy first met Burns in Mauchline in 1785. Just 17 years of age and already a beauty, she inspired Burns to write the song 'Young Peggy' as a tribute to her. At that point in her life she was already involved with McDowall and some time later after a 'secret ceremony' arranged by him, she believed they were married.

In 1794 she gave birth to their daughter at the same time as McDowall inherited his father's estates. He suddenly had the marriage declared unlawful and proceeded to marry the daughter of a wealthy Dumfriesshire laird. An ambitious man, McDowall was already the MP for Wigton by the age of 25, and now a prosperous alliance with another wealthy family in the district was no more than expedient.

In a court battle in 1795 Peggy tried to have their marriage legalised and so legitimise their daughter, but she died before the court could come to a decision. Three years later the Constitutional Court of the Church formally recognised the marriage, but we can only imagine how McDowall managed to have this overruled in the Court of Session. Their daughter, however, was awarded the sum of £3,000, a huge amount in those days, in solatium for her mother's ordeal.

Burns must have had a sixth sense about Peggy Kennedy. In his original letter to her, alongside the song 'Young Peggy', he had wished her good fortune and hoped 'that the snares of villainy never beset you in the road of life'. His song is an everlasting reminder of her suffering and McDowall's treachery.

The Banks o' Doon
Tune – Caledonian Hunt's Delight

Ye banks and braes o' bonie Doon,
How can ye bloom sae fresh and fair!
How can ye chant, ye little birds,
And I sae weary fu' o' care!
Thou'll break my heart, thou warbling bird
That wantons thro' the flowering thorn:
Thou minds me o' departed joys,
Departed, never to return.

Aft hae I rov'd by bonie Doon,
To see the rose and woodbine twine;
And ilka bird sang o' its luve,   *every*
And fondly sae did I o' mine;
Wi' lightsome heart I pu'd a rose,
Fu' sweet upon its thorny tree;
And my fause luver staw my rose,   *false*
But ah! he left the thorn wi' me.

WILLIE BREW'D A PECK O' MAUT

While staying at Moffat in Dumfriesshire in
September 1787, Burns's friend William Nicol
had his peace disturbed by Burns and Allan
Masterton. With the help of generous quantities of
old John Barleycorn they turned his quiet evening into
a night of mindless merriment. To commemorate the
occasion, Burns and Masterton set to work producing this
song, with Burns writing the lyrics and Masterton providing
the tune.

Willie brew'd a Peck o' Maut

O Willie brew'd a peck o' maut,   *malt*
And Rob and Allan cam to pree;   *taste*
Three blyther hearts, that lee-lang night,   *livelong*
Ye wad na found in Christendie.

Chorus –   We are na fou, we're nae that fou,   *full*
But just a drappie on our e'e;   *drop – eye*
The cock may craw, the day may daw,   *dawn*
And ay we'll taste the barley bree.   *brew, juice*

Here are we met, three merry boys,
Three merry boys, I trow, are we;
And mony a night we've merry been,
And mony mae we hope to be!   *more*

It is the moon, I ken her horn,

That's blinkin' in the lift sae hie;   *heavens – high*
She shines sae bright to wyle us hame,   *lure*
But, by my sooth, she'll wait a wee!   *a while*

Wha first shall rise to gang awa,
A cuckold, coward loun is he!   *fellow*
Wha last beside his chair shall fa',
He is the King amang us three!

A RED, RED ROSE

Written in 1794 this song is one of the all-time
favourites for the Burns Supper. By combining a lover's
parting song he found in an old anthology with a
farewell written by a Lieutenant Hinches to his
sweetheart, Burns has produced a lasting
testament to the pain of parting.

A Red, Red Rose
Tune – Graham's Strathspey

O my Luve's like a red, red rose
That's newly sprung in June;
O my Luve's like the melodie
That's sweetly play'd in tune.
As fair art thou, my bonie lass,
So deep in luve am I;
And I will luve thee still, my dear,
Till a' the seas gang dry.

Till a' the seas gang dry, my Dear,
And the rocks melt wi' the sun;
O I will love thee still, my dear,
While the sands o' life shall run.
And fare thee weel, my only Luve!
And fare thee weel a while!
And I will come again, my Luve,
Tho' it were ten thousand mile!

TO A MOUSE

One of his best works and a must for most suppers, this poem shows Burns's
sympathies extending beyond mankind to all his fellow creatures trying to
overcome the frailty of existence. With simplicity and
tenderness he demonstrates his empathy for
the mouse and its new-found
homelessness and reflects on similar
feelings and experiences of his
own. The well-known proverb
from the poem, 'The best-laid
schemes o' Mice an' Men gang
aft a-gley' sums up his
conclusions about life.

The incident which inspired the
poem happened in November 1785,
when Burns ploughed up a mouse's nest and only
just managed to stop John Blane, the boy driving the horses, from killing
his 'fellow-mortal'.

To a Mouse
On turning her up in her nest, with the plough,
November 1785

Wee, sleekit, cowrin, tim'rous beastie,   *sleek*
O, what a panic's in thy breastie!
Thou need na start awa sae hasty,
Wi' bickering brattle!   *hasty scamper*
I wad be laith to rin an' chase thee,   *loath*
Wi' murd'ring pattle!

I'm truly sorry Man's dominion
Has broken Nature's social union,
An' justifies that ill opinion,
Which makes thee startle,
At me, thy poor, earth-born companion,
An' fellow-mortal!

I doubt na, whyles, but thou may thieve;   *sometimes*
What then? poor beastie, thou maun live!
A daimen icker in a thrave   *ear of corn - bundle*
'S a sma' request:
I'll get a blessin wi' the lave,   *remainder*
And never miss't!

Thy wee bit housie, too, in ruin!
Its silly wa's the win's are strewin!
An' naething, now, to big a new ane,   *erect*
O' foggage green!   *moss*
An' bleak December's winds ensuin,
Baith snell and keen!   *biting*

Thou saw the fields laid bare an' waste,
An' weary Winter comin fast,
An' cozie here, beneath the blast,   *comfortable*
Thou thought to dwell,
Till crash! the cruel coulter past
Out thro' thy cell.

That wee bit heap o' leaves an' stibble,   *stubble*
Has cost thee mony a weary nibble!
Now thou's turn'd out, for a' thy trouble,
But house or hald,   *Without – holding*
To thole the Winter's sleety dribble,   *endure – dribble*
An' cranreuch cauld!   *hoar-frost*

But Mousie, thou art no thy lane,   *not alone*
In proving foresight may be vain:
The best-laid schemes o' Mice an' Men
Gang aft a-gley,   *go often wrong*
An' lea'e us nought but grief and pain,   *leave*
For promis'd joy.

Still thou art blest, compar'd wi' me!
The present only toucheth thee:
But, Och! I backward cast my e'e,
On prospects drear!
An' forward, tho' I canna see,
I guess an' fear!

THE RIGS O' BARLEY

This well-known song comes from Burns's early years at Lochlie Farm. His
neighbour, John Rankine, at Adamhill Farm, had a daughter called Annie,

who always maintained she was the heroine of the song, but most of the Annies in the district said the same. Burns believed the last verse to be the best he had ever written, coming nearest to his idea of 'poetical perfection'. A celebration of the rural pleasures of midsummer, it seems essentially Burns.

The Rigs o' Barley
Tune – Corn Riggs

Chorus –

Corn Riggs, an' barley riggs,
An' corn riggs are bonie:
I'll ne'er forget that happy night,
Amang the riggs wi' Annie.

It was upon a Lammas night,
When corn riggs are bonie,
Beneath the moon's unclouded light,
I held awa to Annie;
The time flew by, wi' tentless heed,
Till 'tween the late and early,
Wi' sma' persuasion she agreed
To see me thro' the barley.

The sky was blue, the wind was still,
The moon was shining clearly;
I set her down, wi' right good will,
Amang the riggs o' barley:
I ken't her heart was a' my ain;
I lov'd her most sincerely;
I kiss'd her owre and owre again,
Amang the riggs o' barley.

I lock'd her in my fond embrace;
Her heart was beating rarely:
My blessings on that happy place,
Amang the riggs o' barley!
But by the moon and stars so bright,
That shone that hour so clearly!
She ay shall bless that happy night
Amang the riggs o' barley.

I hae been blythe wi' comrades dear;
I hae been merry drinking;
I hae been joyfu' gath'rin gear;
I hae been happy thinking:
But a' the pleasures e'er I saw,
Tho' three times doubl'd fairly —
That happy night was worth them a'
Amang the riggs o' barley.

BRUCE TO HIS MEN AT BANNOCKBURN

In 1314 King Edward II's 18,000 strong army was resoundingly defeated by Robert the Bruce's 8000 men at the Battle of Bannockburn. Burns composed this imaginary address by Bruce to his soldiers on the morning of the battle, setting it to the air 'Hey tuttie, taitie', believed to be Bruce's marching tune. Burns said it often moved him to tears. He visited the site of the battle in 1787 and visualised his 'gallant, heroic countrymen, coming o'er the hill and down upon the plunderers of their country'.

Burns composed the song in September 1793 and sent it to George Thomson for his *Select Scottish Airs*. Thomson persuaded him to change the tune to 'Lewie Gordon', but public demand ensured that Burns's original choice was reinstated.

Bruce to his Men at Bannockburn
Tune — Hey, tuttie, taitie

Scots, wha hae wi' Wallace bled, *who have*
Scots, wham Bruce has aften led, *whom*
Welcome to your gory bed
Or to victorie!

Now's the day, and now's the hour;
See the front of battle lour;
See approach proud Edward's power —
Chains and slaverie!

Wha will be a traitor-knave?
Wha can fill a coward's grave?
Wha sae base as be a slave?
Let him turn and flee!

Wha for Scotland's king and law
Freedom's sword will strongly draw,
Freeman stand, or freeman fa',
Let him follow me!

By oppression's woes and pains!
By your sons in servile chains!
We will drain our dearest veins,
But they shall be free!

Lay the proud usurpers low!
Tyrants fall in ev'ry foe!
Liberty's in ev'ry blow! –
Let us do or die!

THE EVENING ENDS

BRIEF SPEECHES OF THANKS

As the evening draws to a close the Chairman has a few final duties to perform. First, he calls on a club member or official to thank all the participants in the festivities. This should include thanking the Chairman himself, the Secretary and all those who took part in the preparations.

'AULD LANG SYNE'

Finally, the Chairman asks the company to stand, link hands and to join in the singing of 'Auld Lang Syne'. Burns added the third and fourth verses to this ancient air, making it universally his own. He composed his version of the song in 1788. Now an international anthem, it is sung at the close of gatherings all over the world. Its charm lies in the easy intimacy and simplicity of the lyrics, the remembrance of old friendships and the desire to be transported back to the days of childhood.

Auld Lang Syne

Should auld acquaintance be forgot,	*old*
And never brought to mind?	
Should auld acquaintance be forgot,	
And auld lang syne	*days of long ago*

THE EVENING ENDS

Chorus —

> For auld lang syne, my dear,
> For auld lang syne,
> We'll tak a cup o' kindness yet,
> For auld lang syne.

And surely ye'll be your pint stowp!   *tankard*
And surely I'll be mine!
And we'll tak a cup o' kindness yet,
For auld lang syne.

We twa hae run about the braes,
And pou'd the gowans fine: *pulled*
But we've wander'd mony a weary fitt,   *many — foot*
Sin' auld lang syne.   *Since*

We twa hae paidl'd in the burn   *waded*
Frae morning sun till dine: *dinner-time*
But seas between us braid hae roar'd   *broad*
Sin' auld lang syne.

And there's a hand, my trusty fiere!   *friend*
And gie's a hand o' thine!   *give*
And we'll tak a right gude willie-waught   *draught*
For auld lang syne.

FINAL DETAILS

At this point, unless a dance is planned for the remainder of the evening, the supper draws to a close and the guests depart having thoroughly enjoyed a unique and uplifting occasion. It remains only for the organisers to send letters of thanks to those participants whose efforts have contributed to the evening's success and inform the local press that the supper has been a lively and enjoyable high point in the community's annual list of events. Community involvement, of course, is very much at the heart of the Burns movement, with the Burns Federation promoting the poet's memory and work through schools, lectures and competitions and the Jean Armour Burns Houses and National Burns Memorial Homes, in the district of Mauchline, providing shelter for those in need of a place to spend their final years. Through endeavours of this kind Burns's thoughts and love of his fellow man are turned into deeds by those who share his concern for the less fortunate. This is his true memorial. For further information contact:

The Burns Federation,
Dick Institute,
Elmbank Avenue,
Kilmarnock KA1 3BU,
Scotland UK.
www.robertburns.org

Mill Vennel, Dumfries (now Burns Street)

QUOTATIONS

The following selection of prose and poetry should prove useful to the speechmaker. The quotations have been organised under the headings of mankind, religion, fortune, the lasses, love, drink, wisdom and Burns's beliefs.

Burns himself was an enthusiastic collector of quotations as his poems and letters demonstrate and the following extract testifies:

> I like to have quotations ready for every occasion. – They give
> one's ideas so pat, and save one the trouble of finding
> expression adequate to one's feelings.

> *(Letter to Agnes McLehose, Edinburgh, 14 January 1788)*

MANKIND

Lord! What is man? What a bustling little bundle of passions, appetites, ideas and fancies!

> (From Gordon Irving, *The Wit of Robert Burns*)

> Ye'll try the world soon, my lad,
> And Andrew dear, believe me,
> Ye'll find mankind an unco squad,   *strange crew*
> And muckle they may grieve ye: *much*
> *(Epistle to a Young Friend)*

Conceal yoursel as weel's ye can   *well*
Frae critical dissection;   *from*
But keek thro' ev'ry other man   *look searchingly*
Wi' sharpen'd, sly inspection.
     (Epistle to a Young Friend)

O ye wha are sae guid yoursel,
Sae pious and sae holy,
Ye've nought to do but mark and tell
Your Neebour's fauts and folly!   *faults*
     (Address to the Unco Guid)

'O Man! while in thy early years,
How prodigal of time!
Mis-spending all thy precious hours,
Thy glorious youthful prime!
     (Man was made to mourn)

They gie the wit of age to youth;
They let us ken oursel;
They make us see the naked truth –
The real guid and ill:
Tho' losses an' crosses
Be lessons right severe,
There's wit there, ye'll get there,
Ye'll find nae other where.
     (Epistle to Davie)

RELIGION

When ranting round in Pleasure's ring   *making merry*
Religion may be blinded;

Or if she gie a random sting,   *give*
It may be little minded;
But when on Life we're tempest-driv'n,
A Conscience but a canker –
A correspondence fix'd wi' Heav'n,
Is sure a noble anchor!
    (Epistle to a Young Friend)

... the Sacramental, Executioner-face of a Kilmarnock Communion
    (To Mrs Dunlop, 1 January 1789)

By the bye, I intend breeding him [Burns's eldest son] up for the Church; and from an innate dexterity in secret Mischief which he possesses and a certain hypocritical gravity as he looks on the consequence, I have no small hopes of him in the sacerdotal line.
    (Letter to Alexander Cunningham, Ellisland, 27 July 1788)

One thing frightens me much: that we are to live for ever, seems too good news to be true. – That we are to enter into a new scene of existence, where exempt from want and pain we shall enjoy ourselves and our friends without satiety or separation – how much would I be indebted to any one who could fully assure me that this were certain fact!
    (Letter to Alexander Cunningham, Ellisland, 14 January 1790)

All my fears and cares are of this world: if there is Another, an honest man has nothing to fear from it.
    (Letter to Alexander Cunningham, Ellisland, 14 February 1790)

L–d hear my earnest cry and pray'r
Against that Presbytry of Ayr!
Thy strong right hand, L–d make it bare
Upo' their heads!
L–d visit them and dinna spare,
For their misdeeds!

(*Holy Willie's Prayer*)

FORTUNE

To catch Dame Fortune's golden smile,
Assiduous wait upon her;
And gather gear by ev'ry wile   *wealth*
That's justify'd by Honor:

(*Epistle to a Young Friend*)

Then sore harass'd, and tir'd at last, with Fortune's vain delusion,
I dropt my schemes, like idle dreams, and came to this conclusion
– The past was bad, and the future hid – its good or ill untried;
But the present hour was in my pow'r, and so I would enjoy it.

(*My Father was a Farmer*)

Fortune has so much forsaken me that she has taught me to live
without her.

(*Letter to Charles Sharpe, Dumfries, 22 April 1791*)

The honest heart that' free frae a'
Intended fraud or guile,
However Fortune kick the ba',   *ball*
Has ay some cause to smile;

(*Epistle to Davie*)

All you who follow wealth and power with unremitting ardour,

The more in this you look for bliss, you leave your view the farther:

Had you the wealth Potosi boasts, or nations to adore you,

A cheerful honest-hearted clown I will prefer before you.

(My Father was a Farmer)

THE LASSES

But gie me a cannie hour at e'en,   *happy*

My arms about my dearie, O;

An' war'ly cares, an' war'ly men,

May a' gae tapsalteerie, O!   *topsyturvy*

(Green grow the Rashes)

Auld Nature swears, the lovely dears

Her noblest work she classes, O:

Her prentice han' she try'd on man,

An' then she made the lasses, O.

(Green grow the Rashes)

The charms o' the min', the langer they shine,   *mind*

The mair admiration they draw, man;

While peaches and cherries, and roses and lilies,

They fade and they wither awa, man.

(The Ronalds of the Bennals)

Tho' women's minds, like winter winds,

May shift, and turn, an' a' that,

The noblest breast adores them maist,   *most*
A consequence I draw that.
> *(Song: For a' That an' a' That)*

When ance life's day draws near the   *once*
gloamin,   *twilight*
Then fareweel vacant, careless roamin;
An' fareweel cheerfu' tankards foamin,
An' social noise:
An' fareweel dear, deluding woman,
The joy of joys!
> *(Epistle to James Smith)*

Awa' wi' your witchcraft o' beauty's alarms,
The slender bit beauty you grasp in your arms;
O gie me the lass that has acres o' charms,
O gie me the lass wi' the weelstockit farms. *well – stocked*
> *(Hey for a Lass wi' a Tocher)*

Lassie wi' the lint-white locks,
Bonie lassie, artless lassie,
Wilt thou wi' me tent the flocks   *herd*
Wilt thou be my Dearie O?
> *(Lassie wi' the Lint-white Locks)*

In my conscience I believe that my heart has been so oft on fire that it is absolutely vitrified! I look on the sex with something like the admiration with which I regard the starry sky in a frosty December night. I admire the beauty of the Creator's workmanship; I am charmed with the wild but graceful eccentricity of their motions and – wish them goodnight.

(To Margaret Chalmers, 21 October 1787)

The Devil, the World and the Flesh, are three formidable foes. The first, I generally try to fly from; the second, Alas! generally flies from me; but the third is my plague, worse than the ten plagues of Egypt.

(To William Nicol, 8 March 1788)

Woman is the **BLOOD-ROYAL** of life: let there be slight degrees of precedency among them, but let them all be sacred.

(To Deborah Duff Davies, 6 April 1793)

LOVE

Till a' the seas gang dry, my Dear,
And the rocks melt wi' the sun;
O I will love thee still, my dear,
While the sands o' life shall run.
And fare thee weel, my only Luve!
And fare thee weel a while!
And I will come again, my Luve,
Tho' it were ten thousand mile!

(A Red, Red Rose)

Flow gently, sweet Afton, among thy green
braes,   *hill - slope*
Flow gently, I'll sing thee a song in thy praise;

My Mary's asleep by thy murmuring stream,
Flow gently, sweet Afton, disturb not her dream.
(Afton Water)

Hers are the willing chains o' love,
By conquering Beauty's sovereign law:
And still my Chloris' dearest charm —
She says she lo'es me best of a'.
(She says she lo'es me Best of A')

Then come, thou fairest of the fair,
Those wonted smiles O let me share;
And by thy beauteous self I swear
No love but thine my heart shall know.
(Fairest Maid on Devon Banks)

Had we never loved sae kindly!
Had we never lov'd sae blindly!
Never met — or never parted,
We had ne'er been broken-hearted.
(Ae Fond Kiss)

Ae fond kiss, and then we sever!
Ae fareweel, Alas, for ever!
Deep in heart-wrung tears I'll pledge thee,
Warring sighs and groans I'll wage thee.
(Ae Fond Kiss)

Misery is like Love; to speak its language truly, the Author
must have felt it.

(From Gordon Irving, *The Wit of Robert Burns*)

DRINK

John Barleycorn was a hero bold,
Of noble enterprise;
For if you do but taste his blood,
'Twill make your courage rise.

(John Barleycorn)

Inspiring bold John Barleycorn!
What dangers thou canst make us scorn!
Wi' tippenny, we fear nae evil;
Wi' usquabae we'll face the devil!   *whisky*

(Tam o' Shanter)

We are na fou, we're nae that fou,   *drunk*
But just a drappie on our e'e   *drop — eye*
The cock may craw, the day may daw,   *dawn*
And ay we'll taste the barley bree.   *brew, juice*

(Willie brew'd a Peck o' Maut)

The clachan yill had made me canty, *village ale — merry*
I was na fou, but just had plenty;   *drunk*
I stacher'd whyles, but yet took   *staggered at times*
    tent ay   *care*
To free the ditches;
An' hillocks, stanes, an' bushes, kenn'd ay
Frae ghasits an' witches.

(Death and Dr Hornbook)

Leeze me on drink! it gies us mair   *Commend me to*
Than either school or college;
It kindles wit, it waukens lear,   *rouses learning*
It pangs us fou o' knowledge   *crams – full*
Be 't whisky-gill or penny-wheep,   *very small beer*
Or ony stronger potion,
It never fails, on drinkin deep,
To kittle up our notion,   *enliven our wits*
By night or day.

                    (The Holy Fair)

See Social-life and Glee sit down,
All joyous and unthinking
Till, quite transmugrify'd, they're grown   *transformed*
Debauchery and Drinking.
              (Address to the Unco Guid)

The Whisky of this country is a most rascally liquor; and by consequence, only drunk by the most rascally part of the inhabitants.

          (Letter to John Tennant Jr, Ellisland, 11 December 1788)

Freedom and whisky gan thegither!   *go together*
Tak aff your dram!
      (The Author's Earnest Cry and Prayer)

WISDOM

Gie me ae spark o' nature's fire,
That's a' the learning I desire;

Then tho' I drudge thro' dub an' mire   *puddles*
At pleugh or cart,
My muse, tho' hamely in attire,
May touch the heart.
                (Epistle to J. Lapraik)

But pleasures are like poppies spread,
You seize the flow'r, its bloom is shed;
Or like the snow falls in the river,
A moment white – then melts for ever;
                (Tam o' Shanter)

Life is all a variorum,
We regard not how it goes;
Let them cant about decorum,
Who have character to lose.
                (The Jolly Beggars)

But human bodies are sic fools,
For a' their colleges an' schools,
That when nae real ills perplex them,
They mak enow themsels to vex them;   *enough*
                (The Twa Dogs)

But Mousie, thou art no thy lane,   *not alone*
In proving foresight may be vain:
The best-laid schemes o' Mice an' Men
Gang aft a-gley,   *go often wrong*
An' lea'e us nought but grief and pain,   *leave*
For promised joy.
                (To a Mouse)

Life is but a Day at most;
Sprung from Night – in Darkness lost:
Hope not Sunshine every hour,
Fear not Clouds will ever lour.
Happiness is but a name,
Make Content and Ease thy aim.
Ambition is a meteor-gleam;
Fame, a restless, idle dream;
(Written in Friars' Carse Hermitage)

If happiness hae not her seat,
An' centre in the breast,
We may be wise, or rich, or great,
But never can be blest;
Nae treasures nor pleasures
Could make us happy lang;
The heart ay's the part ay   *always*
That makes us right or wrang.
(Epistle to Davie)

Life is a fairy scene; almost all that deserves the name of
enjoyment, or pleasure, is only charming delusion; and in comes
ripening Age, in all the gravity of hoary wisdom, and wickedly
chases away the deer, bewitching Phantoms.
(To Capt. Richard Brown, 24 February 1788)

BURNS'S BELIEFS

A Mathematician without Religion is a probable character; an irreligious Poet is a Monster.

> (Letter to Mrs Dunlop, Edinburgh, 12 February 1788)

Those who think that composing a Scotch song is a trifling business – let them try.

> (Letter to James Hoy, 6 November 1787)

Whatever mitigates the woes, or increases the happiness of others, this is my criterion of goodness; and whatever injures society at large, or an individual in it, this is my measure of iniquity.

> (Letter to Mrs Dunlop, Edinburgh, 22 June 1789)

In concluding your speech you could use this quote:

I have ever observed that when once people who have nothing to say have fairly set out, they know not when to stop.

> (Letter to Robert Maxwell, Ellisland, 20 Deccmber 1789).

BIBLIOGRAPHY

Chambers, Robert, *The Life and Works of Robert Burns,* Vols I–IV, Chambers, Edinburgh, 1896

Crawford, Thomas, *Burns: A Study of the Poems and Songs,* Oliver and Boyd, Edinburgh, 1960

Daiches, David, *Robert Burns and his World,* Thames and Hudson, London, 1971

DeLancey Ferguson, J. (ed), *The Letters of Robert Burns,* Vols I–II, Oxford University Press, Oxford, 1931

DeLancey Ferguson, J., *Pride and Passion,* Oxford University Press, Oxford, 1939

Irving, Gordon, (ed), *The Wit of Robert Burns,* Leslie Frewin Publications, London, 1972

Jack, Ronald D.S. and Andrew Noble (eds), *The Art of Robert Burns,* Vision Press, London, 1982

Keith, Christina, *The Russet Coat,* Robert Hale, London, 1956

Mackay, James A., *The Burns Federation 1885-1995,* The Burns Federation, Kilmarnock, 1985

Mackay, James A., *A Biography of Robert Burns,* Mainstream Publishing, Edinburgh 1992

Snyder, Franklyn Bliss, *The Life of Robert Burns,* Macmillan, London, 1932

INDEX